Robert Guédiguian

Manchester University Press

DIANA HOLMES AND ROBERT INGRAM *Series editors*
DUDLEY ANDREW *Series consultant*

FRENCH FILM DIRECTORS

Chantal Akerman MARION SCHMID
Auterism from Assayas to Ozon: Five Directors KATE INCE
Jean-Jacques Beineix PHIL POWRIE
Luc Besson SUSAN HAYWARD
Bertrand Blier SUE HARRIS
Catherine Breillat DOUGLAS KEESEY
Robert Bresson KEITH READER
Laurent Cantet MARTIN O'SHAUGHNESSY
Leos Carax GARIN DOWD AND FERGUS DALY
Marcel Carné JONATHAN DRISKELL
Claude Chabrol GUY AUSTIN
Henri-Georges Clouzot CHRISTOPHER LLOYD
Jean Cocteau JAMES S. WILLIAMS
Jacques Demy DARREN WALDRON
Claire Denis MARTINE BEUGNET
Marguerite Duras RENATE GÜNTHER
Julien Duvivier BEN MCCANN
Jean Epstein CHRISTOPHE WALL-ROMANA
Georges Franju KATE INCE
Jean-Luc Godard DOUGLAS MORREY
Mathieu Kassovitz WILL HIGBEE
Diane Kurys CARRIE TARR
Patrice Leconte LISA DOWNING
Louis Malle HUGO FREY
Chris Marker SARAH COOPER
Georges Méliès ELIZABETH EZRA
Negotiating the Auteur JULIA DOBSON
François Ozon ANDREW ASIBONG
Marcel Pagnol BRETT BOWLES
Maurice Pialat MARJA WAREHIME
Jean Renoir MARTIN O'SHAUGHNESSY
Alain Resnais EMMA WILSON
Jacques Rivette DOUGLAS MORREY AND ALISON SMITH
Alain Robbe-Grillet JOHN PHILLIPS
Eric Rohmer DEREK SCHILLING
Coline Serreau BRIGITTE ROLLET
Bertrand Tavernier LYNN ANTHONY HIGGINS
André Téchiné BILL MARSHALL
François Truffaut DIANA HOLMES AND ROBERT INGRAM
Agnès Varda ALISON SMITH
Jean Vigo MICHAEL TEMPLE

Robert Guédiguian

JOSEPH MAI

Manchester University Press

Copyright © Joseph Mai 2017

The right of Joseph Mai to be identified as the author of this work has been asserted by him in accordance with the Copyright, Designs and Patents Act 1988.

Published by Manchester University Press
Oxford Road, Manchester M13 9PL
www.manchesteruniversitypress.co.uk

British Library Cataloguing-in-Publication Data
A catalogue record for this book is available from the British Library

Library of Congress Cataloging-in-Publication Data applied for

ISBN 978 0 7190 9647 1 hardback
ISBN 978 1 5261 6397 4 paperback

First published 2017
Paperback published 2022

The publisher has no responsibility for the persistence or accuracy of URLs for any external or third-party internet websites referred to in this book, and does not guarantee that any content on such websites is, or will remain, accurate or appropriate.

Typeset by Out of House Publishing

Contents

LIST OF PLATES	*page* vi
SERIES EDITORS' FOREWORD	vii
ACKNOWLEDGEMENTS	ix
1 **Living with friends**	1
2 **Fragile friendships: films of the 1980s**	19
3 **Crossing every barrier: the decade of the *conte de L'Estaque***	47
4 **Themes and variation: films since 2000**	85
5 **Conclusion: another cinema – a project in time**	135
FILMOGRAPHY	143
SELECT BIBLIOGRAPHY	151
INDEX	153

Plates

1	Gérard Meylan as Gilbert in *Dernier été*	*page* 80
2	Ariane Ascaride in *Au fil d'Ariane*	80
3	Jean-Pierre Darroussin in his taxi in *La Ville est tranquille*	81
4	Gérard Meylan and Ariane Ascaride in *Dernier été*	81
5	Gérard Meylan, Ariane Ascaride, Jean-Pierre Darroussin and Pierre Banderet in *Ki lo sa?*	82
6	The meal at the end of *À la vie, à la mort!*	82
7	Ariane Ascaride, Pascale Roberts and Frédérique Bonnal in the courtyard in *Marius et Jeannette*	83
8	The Caronte Viaduct in *Dieu vomit les tièdes*	83
9	The beach ball and L'Estaque	84
10	The demolition of the factory	84

All figures provided courtesy of Agat Films & Cie. Cover image courtesy of Francis Blaise and Agat Films & Cie.

Series editors' foreword

To an anglophone audience, the combination of the words 'French' and 'cinema' evokes a particular kind of film: elegant and wordy, sexy but serious – an image as dependent upon national stereotypes as is that of the crudely commercial Hollywood blockbuster, which is not to say that either image is without foundation. Over the past two decades, this generalised sense of a significant relationship between French identity and film has been explored in scholarly books and articles and has entered the curriculum at university level and, in Britain, at A Level. The study of film as art form and (to a lesser extent) as industry has become a popular and widespread element of French Studies, and French cinema has acquired an important place within Film Studies. Meanwhile, the growth in multiscreen and 'art-house' cinemas, together with the development of the video industry, has led to the greater availability of foreign-language films to an English-speaking audience. Responding to these developments, this series is designed for students and teachers seeking information and accessible but rigorous critical study of French cinema and for the enthusiastic filmgoer who wants to know more.

The adoption of a director-based approach raises questions about auteurism. A series that categorises films not according to period or to genre (for example) but to the person who directed them runs the risk of espousing a romantic view of film as the product of solitary inspiration. On this model, the critic's role might seem to be that of discovering continuities, revealing a necessarily coherent set of themes and motifs that correspond to the particular genius of the individual. This is not our aim: the auteur perspective on film, itself most clearly articulated in France in the early 1950s, will be interrogated in certain volumes of the series, and, throughout, the director will be treated as one highly significant element in a complex process of film production and reception that includes socio-economic and political determinants, the work of a large and highly skilled team of artists and technicians, the mechanisms of production and distribution and the complex and multiply determined responses of spectators.

The work of some of the directors in the series is already well known outside France, that of others is less so – the aim is both to provide informative and original English-language studies of established figures and to extend the range of French directors known to anglophone students of cinema. We intend the series to contribute to the promotion of the formal and informal study of French films and to the pleasure of those who watch them.

DIANA HOLMES
ROBERT INGRAM

Acknowledgements

I would like to thank the following people: the series editors, Diana Holmes and Robert Ingram, whose suggestions have greatly improved this manuscript; Martin O'Shaughnessy and Rosemarie Scullion, who kindly read early versions of the project; and Michael Gott, who invited me to share my work on Guédiguian in a keynote address at the University of Cincinnati and who also commented on parts of the manuscript. Moreover, I thank Michael and his co-editor Todd Herzog for permission to include material from my chapter on *Voyage en Arménie* in *East, West and Centre: Reframing Post-European Cinema since 1989* (2015). I am also indebted to Clément Bancel and Julie Rhône at Agat Films & Cie for their prompt and precious aid in procuring images and permissions. In addition, I extend my thanks to Clemson University for a semester of sabbatical leave, during which much of the manuscript was written, and to my home department for supporting a research stay in Marseilles.

This book is to a large extent about the friendships at the heart of Robert Guédiguian's cinema. Its central idea came to me during several extraordinary conversations about the philosophy of friendship with my own friend and colleague, Todd May, to whom I express an enormous debt of gratitude. I reserve my greatest thanks for my closest friend, Tatjana Mai-Wyss, for sharing her insight, good humour and strength, day in and day out.

1

Living with friends

> 'Le cinéma ne m'intéresse pas comme métier: c'est une façon de vivre en collectif.'[1]
>
> (Danel 2008: 95)
>
> 'Que ce soit la politique, les échecs, les boules, le tricot, la pêche à la ligne, le bricolage ou le cinéma, il faut une pratique pour rester amis très longtemps, c'est indispensable: il faut du grain à moudre.'[2]
>
> (Danel 2008: 47)
>
> 'Mais, lorsque nous nous retrouvons, se met en place en un clin d'œil une communauté étonnante, un moment d'utopie où nous allons à nouveau confronter notre histoire à l'Histoire, c'est-à-dire continuer à vivre.'[3]
>
> (Danel 2008: 46)

Robert Guédiguian has had an industrious and productive career lasting thirty-five years (and counting), producing, co-writing and directing nineteen full-length films, as well as a parallel career as an independent film producer with Agat Films & Cie, a company that he co-founded in the early 1990s. His work attracts a core of loyal fans, numbering approximately 200,000, who consistently turn out for

---

[1] 'The cinema does not interest me as a craft: it is a way of living collectively.' Unless otherwise stated, all translations are mine.
[2] 'Whether it is politics, chequers, boules, knitting, fishing, fixing things around the house, or the cinema, you need a practice in order to stay friends for a long time, it's indispensable. You need grist for the mill.'
[3] 'However, whenever we meet up, an amazing community is instantly re-established, a moment of utopia, in which we can once again confront our story with History, which is to say, to continue to live.'

every film he releases. His most successful film, *Marius et Jeannette* (1997), attracted over 2.5 million viewers in France, had worldwide success and can be considered a key film of its decade.[4]

And yet, Guédiguian insists, as he does in the above citations (typical of many statements he has made over the years, and so to be taken seriously), that he really does not care so much about the cinema, that it does not interest him as a career or as a craft but as a practice with another goal: to enable friends to 'live together'. The critical reception of his work may reflect this ambivalence: though he has many defenders, he also has a number of detractors who find his work too ideological, too simplistic, too Manichean, too melodramatic, etc. Guédiguian has sometimes been criticised for making 'fictions de gauche', well-intentioned leftist narratives that argue for a different world while neglecting to imagine a different cinema. The charge may or may not have some justification in the case of some individual films, but it is blind to the profoundly original and durable project of 'living together' that underpins Guédiguian's work and that constitutes a truly different cinema. In this book, I will discuss all of Guédiguian's films to date, sometimes in great detail, but I will do so with an eye to developing this deeper project. Indeed, much of their aesthetic merit, it seems to me, will appear more evident once it comes into focus.

L'Estaque, political commitment and the Common Programme

Living with friends, to 'remain together for a long time', involves a particular practice that I hope to explain over the course of this introduction. But it also has to do with 'newly confronting our story with History'. On one hand, as we will see, this means that friendships are self-aware. On the other hand, the capitalisation of 'History' should tip us off that Guédiguian has a view of history related to Marxism. For Guédiguian, history, as Marx argues in *The German Ideology*, begins with life, the 'real individuals, their activity and the material conditions under which they live, both those which

---

4 Most of the films since *Marius et Jeannette* have had between the core 200,000 and 400,000 viewers, with as many as 600,000 for *Les Neiges du Kilimandjaro*.

they find already existing and those produced by their activity' (Marx 1983: 163). Human life is moulded by these conditions, but humans also act upon the world to produce new conditions for living. When there is a contradiction in the ways in which the means of subsistence are produced, for example, when the social organisation of feudalism no longer reflects an economy in which the bourgeoisie is the main producer of wealth, then a revolution takes place – thesis gives way to antithesis – and a new synthesis is, at least provisionally, put into place. Guédiguian is a film-maker from the working class, and so 'living with friends' involves, for him, a constant evaluation of friendship from an outside perspective, in light of the place of this class within History.[5] These two strands of friendship will be at the centre of this book: friendship as a local story and friendship within a broader, collective History.

This understanding of 'living' in history is anchored in Guédiguian's own upbringing, in L'Estaque (and surrounding areas), the working-class neighbourhood of Marseilles where he was born and raised and where most of his films are set. L'Estaque, today forming a somewhat isolated northern neighbourhood of the city, sits on a bay surrounded by rocky hills, protected from the strong Mediterranean winds: the Provençal word 'Estaca' refers to floating landing stages in the bay where passing vessels sought shelter in bad weather. (The word's literal meaning, 'attachment', rings true to many of Guédiguian's thematic concerns.) L'Estaque has been inhabited since prehistoric times, served as a port for loading wine during antiquity and later became a small hamlet of peasants and fishermen, though eventually the mackerel, sardines and sea urchins will have disappeared.

Émile Zola's 1884 novella *Naïs Micoulin* reads like a sepia photograph of the village during the transformations of an industrial revolution characterised by toil and class divisions. Zola tells the story of two lovers: Frédéric Rostand, the son of a wealthy lawyer from Aix, and Naïs, a beautiful young peasant girl whose father is the caretaker of the Rostand family's country estate in L'Estaque. In an earlier period, Micoulin would have been a fisherman, and he still supplements his table with excursions into the bay to check his traps, but the family's way of life is disappearing, and his daughter Naïs

---

5 I will retain Guédiguian's capitalisation throughout whenever I am referring to this view of history.

must take a job in one of the new cement factories in town. Frédéric, who has known Naïs since childhood, becomes infatuated when she becomes a young woman; at night the two sit on rocks looking out at Marseilles at the other end of the bay. Micoulin discovers the affair and plots to kill Frédéric, but he is killed in the process, when a chance bolt of lightning causes a landslide in the ground that he has weakened by creating an irrigation system for the olive trees. (Modernity kills him.) Frédéric, though a bourgeois and becoming a lawyer, comports himself as a kind of village lord. An injustice is expressed in gendered power relationships in a way that announces many of Guédiguian's narratives: he soon tires of Naïs and abandons her; she marries a hunchback from the factory and grows old and ugly. Zola's story bears witness to rapidly disappearing, centuries-old work traditions – fishing and agriculture – rapidly transformed through modern, capitalistic industrial techniques.

Characters in Guédiguian's films still set out on a fishing excursion from time to time, in an evocation of antique L'Estaque. But his films are, of course, usually set in the stages of late capitalism, when the factories themselves are being torn down, as can be seen famously in *Marius et Jeannette*. In the late nineteenth and early twentieth centuries, L'Estaque experienced an influx of immigrants who came to work in these factories, following a promise of a better life, mainly from Italy, Spain, Algeria and Armenia, that would increase its population from a few hundred early in the twentieth century to 13,000 by 1931. Construction of canals, the Estaque train station and the viaduct of Corbière linked the town more closely to Marseilles. For many years L'Estaque remained a seaside resort known for its beach, village atmosphere and cuisine. At the same time, a neighbourhood like Les Riaux, built on housing allotments surrounding the factories, contrasted starkly with the few bourgeois homes of the village. This period also saw a rise in labour organisation and Communist Party activity. L'Estaque fell on hard times, however, after the Second World War, during recession, decolonisation and globalisation. Tile factories began to close, the bay was depleted of fish, shanty towns near factories started to appear in the empty lots made available by factory owners. Skilled labour jobs disappeared overseas; most factories were gone by the 1970s. *Rouge midi* attempts to tell much of this history. Even in 2015, while L'Estaque enjoys something of a third life with tourism, unemployment stands at over 16 per cent.

Guédiguian was born during the early days of L'Estaque's decline, in 1953, though he has fairly recent foreign origins. His paternal grandfather was an Armenian who had come to France to study theology and stayed in Marseilles, eventually giving help to the influx of Armenians escaping genocide in Turkey. His mother came from a Catholic, anti-Nazi family in Germany, where she had met Guédiguian's father in 1943, when he was stationed for obligatory work at a hospital near Cologne in the STO (Service du Travail Obligatoire) during the Second World War. At the same time, the first and strongest sense of significant group identification for Guédiguian did not come from national origins but from class and the Communist Party. Guédiguian's mother worked as a housecleaner and stay-at-home mother, his father as an electrician on the docks; they voted communist but were not politically militant. Guédiguian observed his parents' difficulties, feared for his own economic future and was politicised from an early age. He also owes a great intellectual and political debt to his childhood friend and future collaborator, Gérard Meylan, whom he had met at age five, when the latter was delivering the communist newspaper *L'Humanité* from door to door with his father.[6] It was while listening to conversations between Meylan's father and uncle (one was a schoolmaster and the other a leader in the Conféderation Générale de Travail, France's largest labor union – Guédiguian compares them to his personal Marx and Engels) that he started to form an understanding of the world.

Guédiguian's political consciousness grew during adolescence as he and Meylan became communist youth organisers. (He is proud that the youth cell he led was the largest in Marseilles.) During May 1968, at age fourteen, the two were organising demonstrations at their high school in Marseilles. Guédiguian eventually would attend the University of Aix-en-Provence to study law and economics and hone his debating skills against the conservative student body that dominated the university. (At the time there was no law school in Marseilles.) A year after meeting Ariane Ascaride in Aix in 1974, Guédiguian followed her to Paris, where he started a thesis at the School for Advanced Studies in the Social Sciences (the EHESS), on the conception of the state in the history of the worker's movement, under the direction of a well-known Marxist historian, Georges

---

6 For a full treatment of Guédiguian's family origins and youth, see Kantcheff 2013: 8–17.

Haupt.[7] History, and historiography with a militant and pedagogical goal, will be central to his cinema as well.

Despite this political commitment, Guédiguian underwent a major personal political crisis in the late 1970s, resulting in his departure from the French Communist Party in 1980. This departure was not unique to him: after decades of growth, the late 1970s and early 1980s were particularly difficult times for communism in France, and the party was in the throes of defeat, for many reasons. There are many ways of looking at the demise of communism in France, but two versions seem relevant here.

One version is perhaps best told by those whom one might consider Haupt's intellectual enemies, the anti-communist historians who took the weakening of the Communist Party for a positive sign of the end of totalitarianism. In his account of what he calls the 'communist illusion', François Furet argues that communism (and fascism) grew out of an historical break from aristocratic societies by which modern societies set forth on a course towards individual freedom and wealth. A new cultural figure is identified, the bourgeois, whose value is asserted through having more wealth than his neighbour. The bourgeois is 'animated by a corpuscular agitation, constantly driving it forward', blazing a self-sustaining path away from the common good, atomising society and turning government into a means of protecting economic interests (Furet 1999: 3). Furet, however, is sceptical of the intellectual fixation on the bourgeois and claims that much anti-bourgeois passion is simply self-hatred of the victorious bourgeoisie itself, torn between the need to protect the new money-based social order and feelings of guilt for having instituted a 'market, not a citizenry' (Furet 1999: 13). For Furet, communism and fascism were totalitarian choices within a much wider array of responses to the modern democratic world. Both begat violent, repressive regimes: in communism, 'Stalin would exterminate millions in the battle against the bourgeoisie' (Furet 1999: 29). Rather than the promise of democracy and the social link, communism

---

7 'C'était mon rêve d'alors de devenir un grand intellectuel au service de la vérité qui, comme on ne devrait jamais l'oublier, est toujours révolutionnaire' (It was my dream at the time to become a great intellectual at the service of the truth, which is, one should never forget, always revolutionary) (Guédiguian 2012: 135).

crudely defended the single-party state of the Soviet Union. This definition of communism as a totalitarianism became ambient among historians of the 1970s and 1980s, partly in reaction to academic historiography, dominated by Marxists such as Haupt. It does reflect the increasing conviction among many that the USSR was a monolithic roadblock to democracy; its fall could only be welcomed.

Since Guédiguian went on to make a film about him, it is important to mention the role played by François Mitterrand in administering the final political blow to communism at the French national level. Mitterrand had opposed communism his whole life but realised that the number of true believers in Stalinism and the French Communist Party was actually quite small and that most of the party's support resulted from anti-bourgeois sentiment and dissatisfaction with Gaullist and other rightist policies. He set out to gain the trust of as many party supporters as possible. This was the period of the 'Common Programme of Government', negotiated in 1972, between the socialists and the communists, which included an official leftist alliance through a shared platform, including mass nationalisations (Tiersky 2000: 111). The Common Programme returns intermittently in Guédiguian's interviews and even in films, including *Les Neiges du Kilimandjaro*, where a union organiser imagines that he has received a copy of it for his wedding anniversary. Mitterrand was never sincerely committed to collaboration with the communists but instead was interested in the electoral influence that the socialist reformers could win in communist strongholds. Eventually the communist leaders sabotaged the Common Programme by making extravagant demands such as 100 per cent state ownership of nationalised enterprises. Ronald Tiersky explains their intentions: 'At a negotiating meeting on September 22, 1977, the Communists achieved their goal, a crack-up of the Union of the Left in which they seemed no more responsible than the Socialists' (2000: 117). But it was too late for them: Mitterrand won the presidency in 1981, and the communists were permanently eclipsed.

No more responsible than the socialists? Here's how Guédiguian remembers the same events:

> We told ourselves we were going to make it! And not three centuries from now – it was there, so close, within reach. And then, in 1975, we entered the period where the Communists and the Socialists

> renegotiated their agreements for municipal elections in 1977 ... and I found myself in disagreement with the Communists. I continued to go to my cell every day, say what I had to say, but it didn't change anything. Then, in September 1977, I will never forget the day in the metro, coming out of the cinema with Gérard (Meylan), we read in *Le Monde* that the negotiations to renew the Common Programme were interrupted. Our deception was total: it was a closing off, a suicidal folding in ... I was certain then as I am now that a few leaders ... killed the Communist Party.
>
> (Danel 2008: 42)

As communism fell apart, Guédiguian's faith in the movement of History ('we were going to make it, and not three centuries from now') was shaken.

But Guédiguian did not share the jubilation of some of the historians at the downfall of communism. Centrist liberal historians, like Furet, seem to warmly embrace the victory of the market economy and the rise of neo-liberalism. Furet's title itself – *Le Passé d'une illusion* (*The Passing of an Illusion*) – has echoes of Francis Fukuyama's 'end of history', whose main thesis asserts that Western liberal democracies no longer have a viable opponent and have become the 'final form of government'. For Guédiguian, however – and this is the second way of looking at it – the fall of communism is tragic: he thus shares the view of those on the left who see this period as the imposition of a new global regime that has been particularly successful at eroding social protections and economic conditions for the working class.

The fall of communism, even partially self-inflicted, took away one major tool for forwarding History. For Martin O'Shaughnessy, the victory of neo-liberalism has reasons that are both positive and negative. On one hand, capitalism had become 'open to networking, creativity, intuition and difference in a way that made the critique of alienation and unfreedom harder to enforce' (O'Shaughnessy 2008: 8).[8] But, on the other hand, there has been a systematic erosion of the institutions of the left and replacement with neo-liberal practices. O'Shaughnessy outlines a labour landscape divided by 'individualisation of awards', job insecurity, subcontracting, flexitime, surveillance

---

8 For Guédiguian, this happens often through the ease with which individuals can acquire credit and mind-numbing access to enhanced consumption (Sahuc 2011: 35).

and other forms of division (O'Shaughnessy 2008: 9). Of course the atrocities of communist states served readily as cover for these moves: the USSR, China and Cambodia had become, even for staunch Marxists like Alain Badiou, 'statist' and had wandered from the front lines of the 'vanguard of history' (O'Shaughnessy 2008: 9). In addition, the Socialist Party, for those on the 'left of the left', like Guédiguian, has turned increasingly to the centre since Mitterrand's election and supported liberal and neo-liberal economic policies. As a result, large portions of the working class were completely marginalised, which in turn eroded values such as solidarity, class identity and collective resistance.

For Guédiguian, no clear political option opened itself up: he did not cling to the party, did not 'reform' himself as a centrist liberal and did not become a socialist. He speaks of many friends and colleagues who became depoliticised (like some of his characters), joined the Human Rights League or turned to union organising (at a time when labour unions were also being emptied of their influence). There was still to be a left, but a left needing to be reinvented, and nobody quite understood how. O'Shaughnessy appropriately situates Guédiguian as a film-maker working within the 'fragments' of leftist identity; Philip Anderson, more pessimistically, calls his vision of history 'apocalyptic'. Guédiguian's response is actually quite original, though its effectiveness will only emerge over time. At the end of Chapter 2 and the beginning of Chapter 3 I will return to Guédiguian's rejection of the point of view of Furet and like-minded historians and his personal redefinition of communism.

The adventure of friendship

I want to draw attention to Guédiguian's mention of Gérard Meylan, present with him in the metro car (coming out of the cinema) when the fatal news of the socialist-communist rift arrived. The detail hints at the second major theme that emerges from Guédiguian's youth, one that is perhaps less immediately visible since it is less frequently cited than ideology as a subject of critical analysis in the cinema: friendship. Consider just a few of the names that will occur throughout this book. The first difference-making friendship in Guédiguian's life was with Meylan, and the two were known as the 'twins' since they were age ten and eleven. The friendship with Meylan survived two very different trajectories when Guédiguian studied in Aix and Meylan enrolled in nursing school in Marseilles: in fact, Meylan continued to work as a hospital nurse, acting during holiday and other types of leave, almost exclusively in Guédiguian's films, until his recent retirement. Others would join this pair. In 1968, while organising, the boys grew close to Malek Hamzaoui over a game of table football in a bar memorialised in *Lady Jane*. Hamzaoui, who appeared in two early films, is now Guédiguian's production manager. Ariane Ascaride would appear on the scene in Aix during Guédiguian's studies, and when Guédiguian followed her to Paris he would meet other future collaborators, Jean-Pierre Darroussin, Pierre Banderet and Jacques Boudet, who would also form part of Guédiguian's core ensemble. (See Chapters 2 and 5 for more details.) Guédiguian was undergoing a 'militant reconversion' (to borrow Tissot's term) from political organisation to the cinema, a career that would not abandon politics but would also be devoted to friendship, ethics and art (see Tissot et al. 2006). Indeed, friendship, in the way Guédiguian represents and explores it, will have important political implications.

It is helpful to consider friendship first as a philosophical notion. This discussion will be far from exhaustive: I merely want to give an idea of a certain type of friendship that seems relevant to Guédiguian's work, for it is valuable for appreciating the stakes involved. One of the most influential philosophical discussions of friendship can be traced back to Aristotle, whose interest in the subject grows out of a broader attempt to define 'happiness', or what he calls more generally *eudaimonia*, in 'actions, arts, and sciences' (Aristotle 2011: 2). Friendship, as Aristotle sees it, is a major part of all areas of a successful human life; indeed, he claims that it is one of the greatest goods that human beings can experience. If Marx wrote about the 'production' of life, Aristotle's account is about the quality or flourishing of life. In Guédiguian's work, friendship will mix with work and politics in a highly original way.

In the *Nicomachean Ethics*, Aristotle divides friendships, or *philia*, into three types: friendships of use, friendships of pleasure and character friendships (sometimes called 'virtue', 'deep' or 'true' friendships). The first two types emphasise the primacy of one's individual self in relationship to others. Friendships of utility, like many business arrangements, are built on the expectation that I will receive, in the future, some direct benefit from someone else. Pleasure friendships offer me immediate enjoyment or the gratification of some desire at this time and this place. Both of these types of friendship imply that the other person is to some extent functional in relation to me. There is a much sharper distinction between these and the third type of friendship. In character or true *philia*, relationships are not based on something I hope to gain for myself in the future or in the present. These friendships are other-oriented: I wish for and celebrate my friends' successes – and feel sorrow at their suffering – for their sake. These types of friendships draw us out of ourselves and towards the other person.[9]

The difference between character friendships and the first two categories is a sign that Aristotle's use of the term *eudaimonia* does not encompass everything we mean when we say 'good' or 'successful'. He does not have in mind a good in which an individual would accrue some direct and present profit or passing pleasure. Instead, Aristotle's view of *eudaimonia* is much more holistic and less definable; it refers to the flourishing of the entire life of a person in all its dimensions. Because of this, we do not enter into deep *philia*, as we might pleasure or utility friendships, because we have calculated some goal or a benefit that will accrue to us. The basic glue that holds together friendships is, as Elizabeth Telfer has argued, passion for the other person, an affection that draws us to who they are, what they say and what they do (see Telfer 1991). Such passion intertwines our life deeply with the lives of our friends, affecting all aspects of our lives.

For example, friendships produce sometimes imperceptible but profound effects on how we experience time, space and action at a basic, daily level. We want to be near our friends and spend our time with them. Much of our life stretches out over fairly empty periods of time that are not organised towards some goal. Friendships can cast a glaze of meaning over these empty periods. But even the accomplishment of important actions involves an interminable series of small, banal efforts. Discussions and collaboration with friends, or just the interest that our friends take in our work, can support us and keep us focused through the boring but necessary details. They

---

9 See Cooper 1980 for a canonical general interpretation of friendship in Aristotle.

can also give us the confidence to confront our weaknesses in the pursuit of something worthwhile (see Cooper 1980). For Alexander Nehamas, this kind of redemption of the quotidian has implications for how time is represented in works of art (Nehamas 2010: 271). If epics and novels have the scope to represent grand actions, a number of elements make cinema, and certainly Guédiguian's cinema, a natural genre for representing the microscopic and seemingly empty units of time at play in friendships. Limited to a couple of hours but with more built-in realism, a film often represents these quotidian moments – car rides, conversations in cafés, family dinners – in order to capture their hidden meaning or to allow the many facets of their more or less dramatic dynamics to unfold. We could make the same point about places and objects. Guédiguian avoids historic or striking settings to give meaning to banal social spaces: apartments, alleys, courtyards, bars, housing estates, etc. Guédiguian's films are also filled with objects – cups of coffee, pieces of clothing, streets, tables, etc. – that receive a layer of meaning because they have made some kind of entry into the dynamic relationships between people.

The deeper our intertwining, the more friendships open us up to latent differences within ourselves. Friendships can provide laboratories for exploring our own values by simple observation of and attention to our friends' better qualities: their beauty, talents and their moral and intellectual acumen. Friends act as analogies for ourselves: what we find valuable in them may help us locate and cultivate our own hidden talents and moral or intellectual qualities. One of the greatest transformative tools of friendship is the serious kind of conversation that Montaigne calls 'de la conférence'. Challenging conversation might not even take place without friendships, since without them we may not develop the deep level of trust necessary to tackle subjects on which we are vulnerable to challenge from other points of view. Guédiguian's films often take place away from dramatic action and around a table, where the characters eat, drink, play cards or table football, observe each other and their surroundings and, most importantly, discuss matters of personal, social and political importance. Sometimes these scenes are accused of being mere *pagnolades*, as in Marcel Pagnol's great *Fanny* trilogy, an obvious influence on Guédiguian but whose conversations are often more narrow and comic. Guédiguian's characters engage in critique and argument about ideas and actions, leading to changes in opinion and the sharpening of critical capacities. Conversation with deep friends thus helps us develop and revise our way of looking at the world.

We can point to how deep friendships affect our outlook on various issues, but, since friendship is a kind of passion, as Telfer has argued, it would be odd to reduce the benefits of friendship to what we can name. Likewise, Nehamas emphasises that what matters to us is not what our friend 'did', but what he 'is, which no list of his features, however long, could ever capture' (2010: 277). For Nehamas this implies a Nietzschean conception of identity, according to which no division can be made between the individual and that individual's separate attributes. Instead of a static identity, this kind of identity grows and changes in friendships, through actions, conversation and a general engagement in life. This is close to Amélia Rorty's definition of friendship as a process of 'dynamic permeability' (1993: 79). Such dynamism makes friendship its own adventure, in which my encounter with this particular friend leads my identity into unforeseen territory. Friendships are 'difference-making' not only in that they matter but also in that they differentiate me from others through my shared narrative with another person.

Therefore, though we can have many friends, each one makes us different in a certain way. Montaigne answers enigmatically when asked why he and Etienne de La Boétie were such close friends: 'par ce que c'estoit luy; par ce que c'estoit moy' (Montaigne 1962: 187).[10] Friendship is about personal and historical particulars, and friends are therefore irreplaceable. Character friendships are not predicated on promises of rewards or instant gratification but on long-term interaction with these particular other people: they link us into a narrative including past, present and future. Rorty again insists on 'constancy' and 'endurance' within change (1993: 73). What underpins Guédiguian's career as a film-maker, and a political militant film-maker, is the narrative (our 'story', he calls it) of a number of friendships that have developed over time. These friendships, these particular and irreplaceable friendships, are primary. This helps explain Guédiguian's frequent comment that he is both 'inside' and 'outside' the cinema. Film-making is grist for the mill of friendship, a necessity for 'remaining friends a long period of time' and a way

---

10 'because it was him, because it was me'.

of 'living together'. Guédiguian's cinema is in many essential ways a monument built to the friendships that make up his life.

Figures and counter-figures: living with friends in the 'Age of Economics'

This turn to friendship at a moment of crisis might look like a renunciation of politics and a retreat to a private sphere. But such a retreat would not be 'living' in the sense of confronting the personal story of the friendship with 'History'. For Guédiguian, friendship is rather an essential part of the search for new forms of politics, a search whose urgency comes through in a response Guédiguian gives to a question about how to 'reconstruct the left': 'par abandonner le rêve sans le trahir, c'est-à-dire le réinventer' (Sahuc 2011: 61).[11] What role might friendship play in such a reinvention?

To see the role that *philia* might play in this reinvention, it is helpful to look at friendship, as does the philosopher Todd May, as a *figure* in contrast with other figures for human interaction. Figures take many forms: they can be images, narratives, debates, legal decisions, practices and other discursive figures that provide examples or paths that encourage people to live or think in certain ways. As May writes, they 'mould' our lives, often in a normative way. They choreograph our movements, structure our time, orient our relations to others and contribute to our self-definition. Often they work on us in an unconscious way, but we can also critique and reject figures, choosing new ones that better reflect our values. However, in an age of neo-liberalism, May points out that the normative figures that dominate economic and cultural forms are those that structure our selves in ways that increase the free flow of capital and assure the unfettered functioning of markets. According to May's analysis, this system proposes two main figures (both of which are highly relevant to Guédiguian's work): the consumer and the entrepreneur.

May analyses both of these figures in three ways: in the relation between individual and the environment; in the relation between the individual and time; and, finally, in the types of self-identification

---

11 'By abandoning the dream without betraying it, which is to say by reinventing it.'

and relationships to others that the figures encourage. The consumer, in contrast, say, to a creator or a producer, has a passive relation to the environment. We consume within the choices of activities and brand names that are laid out before us. As we consume, we are unconcerned with the past or the future but focused on what is going on around us right now: we are caught up in the moment, in our pleasure, in our entertainment, and, when instant gratification is fulfilled, we move on to another activity, another point in time. May calls this a pointillist relation to time. In turn, the present is redefined as that space of time that is somehow obliged to grant me gratification: any other experience of time seems without value.[12] Finally, as consumers, we are focused on our self, on our pleasure. A consumer has little empathy or concern for others and does not identify with a larger group.

More active than the consumer, the entrepreneur looks at life 'in terms of calculative self-enhancement' (May 2014: 54): the entrepreneur thinks, either explicitly or implicitly, in terms of rational investment. This way of thinking colours our choice of actions as we set goals, consider possible courses of action and make decisions based on how those actions will help or hinder our goals. Other people enter into our calculations as possible investments: will spending time with this person further my goals in an efficient way or not? Indeed, the entrepreneur will even consider his or her own self as 'human capital' to be developed according to some goal. May distinguishes between using this rationality to achieve goals that may be very diverse, and even altruistic, from their application in a strictly neo-liberal context in which, according to influential neo-liberal economic theorists such as Milton Friedman, altruism plays no role (May 2014: 47). The figure of the entrepreneur, then, encourages us to be active in relation to our environment, future-oriented and, once again, individualistic, despite any moral arguments to the contrary.

These two figures, it should be clear, map easily onto Aristotle's first two definitions of friendship relationships. Consumers, to the extent that they need other people at all, see them as providers of entertainment or objects of consumption, or at best, as in Aristotle's

12 One might add another dimension of time to the consumer, which May omits, a relation to the future, for much of contemporary consumption now creates debt, and the consumer's thoughts about the future may be accompanied by a vague dread.

pleasure friendships, they share some superficial, temporary pleasures. As in utility friendships, the entrepreneur enters into commerce with others in order to further his or her chances of reaching a particular goal. Neither figure includes a passion for the other as an end and everything that entails. As we have seen, Guédiguian responds to the ascendency of the entrepreneur and the consumer by making the cinema an activity for living with friends, for a long time. His practice stands outside of industrial practices (through independent self-production) as a kind of heterotopia against the predominant figures of neo-liberalism. Friendship is a practice giving meaning to our lives, but it also has a stake in politics. For Guédiguian, in the age of economics, it is the anti-bourgeois figure par excellence.

Guédiguian's project is both practical and discursive: his friends are sharing a life together, but they are producing images of *philia* that they propose to viewers as figures for our own possible adoption. In terms of narrative, Guédiguian's films usually look something like this: a group of friends, in economic difficulties during a time of eroding class identity and waning political leverage, works together to preserve their relationships and solidarity. Their tone ranges from comic, as friends come together to eat, drink and make jokes, to tragic, when friendships are forced to end. In terms of image, Guédiguian's work is infused with a beautiful if realistic luminosity and colour, a camera whose supple movement follows the interactions of the characters, and editing that often reflects the situation of the friends in their stage of History.

Friendships are like strands of thread combining with others to become a fabric, with a certain design or shape, worn no matter where one goes, what one does or what one thinks. They give Guédiguian's work the feel of a coherent project from start to end. But when Guédiguian made the conversion from historian and 'communist intellectual' to film-maker working with friends, he was probably not aware of how long this project would last or how rich it would be. This book follows its development chronologically. Chapter 2 examines Guédiguian's first four films, in which the viewer discovers many facets of the experience of friendship. These films establish not only the particulars of space (L'Estaque and nearby places) and people (Guédiguian's core actors and technicians) but also their struggles as history shifts from class struggle to post-communist neo-liberalism. A reflection of the 1980s, these films end pessimistically, in the permanent separation of the friends, in displacement or, most often, in death. In the films dealt with in Chapter 3, perhaps Guédiguian's most original work, friendships rise above these socio-political constraints in what he calls the *conte de L'Estaque*: instead of political impotence, these films offer a new model for political action, a model that is local, affective and utopian. By the time we reach the films made since 2000, treated in Chapter 4, friendships are deeply woven into the fabric of Guédiguian's cinematic and political life. These films explore more variety, in genre, geographical space, historical period and figures of identification. I will take advantage of the conclusion in Chapter 5 to step outside of individual films and examine Guédiguian's career as a whole, as an ongoing and cohesive project, and consider what makes it original, durable and valuable.

References

Anderson, Philip (2008) 'Stories of Violence, Violence of History: The Political Logic of Guédiguian's Cinema from *Dernier été* (1980) to *La Ville est tranquille* (2001)', *The Australian Journal of French Studies*, 45:3, 238–49.
Aristotle (2011) *Nichomachean Ethics*, Chicago, Ill.: University of Chicago Press.
Cooper, John M. (1980) 'Aristotle on Friendship', in Amélie Oksenberg Rorty (ed.), *Essays on Aristotle's Ethics*, Berkeley, Calif.: University of California Press, pp. 301–40.
Danel, Isabelle (2008) *Conversation avec Robert Guédiguian*, Paris: Les Carnets de l'Info.
Fukuyama, Francis (1992) *The End of History and the Last Man*, New York: Free Press.
Furet, François (1999) *The Passing of an Illusion*, Chicago, Ill.: University of Chicago Press.
Guédiguian, Robert (2012) 'L'Historien au cœur conscient', *Cahiers Jaurès*, 1:203, 135–6.
Kantcheff, Christophe (2013) *Robert Guédiguian, cinéaste*, Paris: Éditions du Chêne.
Marx, Karl (1983) *The Portable Karl Marx*, New York: Penguin.
May, Todd (2014) *Friendship in an Age of Economics*, Lanham, Md.: Lexington Books.
Montaigne, Michel de (1962) *Œuvres complètes*, Paris: Gallimard.
Nehamas, Alexander (2010) 'The Good of Friendship', *Proceedings of the Aristotelian Society*, 110:3, 267–94.
O'Shaughnessy, Martin (2008) *The New Face of Political Cinema*, New York: Berghahn Books.

Rorty, Amélia (1993) 'The Historicity of Psychological Attitudes: Love Is Not Love Which Alters Not When It Alteration Finds', in Neera Kapur Badhwar (ed.), *Friendship: A Philosophical Reader*, Ithaca, NY: Cornell University Press.

Sahuc, Stéphane (2011) *Parlons politique: Maryse Dumas-Robert Guédiguian*, Paris: Les Éditions Arcane-17.

Telfer, Elizabeth (1991) 'Friendship', in Michael Pakaluk (ed.), *Other Selves: Philosophers on Friendship*, Indianapolis, Ind.: Hackett, pp. 248–67.

Tierksy, Ronald (2000) *François Mitterrand: The Last French President*, New York: St Martin's Press.

Tissot, Sylvie, Christophe Gaubert and Marie-Hélène Lechien (eds.) (2006) *Reconversions militantes*, Limoges: Pulim.

Zola, Émile (2015) *Naïs Micoulin et autres nouvelles*, Paris: Hatie.

2

Fragile friendships
Films of the 1980s

One cannot make the claim that the four films Guédiguian made during the 1980s were commercial successes. They did, however, receive critical praise and are worth viewing and reflection for many reasons. Most of all, they launch Guédiguian's project of making films collectively, with friends, especially actors whose bodies are introduced to viewers and will remain during all of Guédiguian's career.[1] They also establish the various spaces of L'Estaque, both private and public, that appear throughout Guédiguian's career: its homes, workplaces, bars, streets, beaches, *criques*, etc. They also introduce us to Guédiguian's recurring characters and groups, the ins and outs of deep friendships (conversation, difference, self-revelation) and the difficulties of preserving friendships in hostile socio-economic circumstances. These difficulties arise when these friendships are considered at their moment in History. The films of the period are a deep reflection of the political crises of the French left during the political and economic realignments of the decade of Reagan, Thatcher, *perestroika* and Mitterrand. Thus, in the 1980s, Guédiguian attempted to work through a contradiction: on the one hand, he explores the goodness of friendship and its way of bestowing meaning on lived experiences; on the other hand, he attempts to exorcise a pessimistic view of the History in which these friendships take form. This latter attempt will be more successful after the 1980s.

---

1 See Mariette 2005 for a full account of Guédiguian's transition from student of history to film-maker, through many encounters with people still active in his career.

Dernier été (1981)

Released in the same year as Luc Besson's *cinéma du look* piece *Diva*, *Dernier été* is a film out of step with the cinema's contemporary trends because of its realistic depiction of working-class people with complex personal lives. Its opening sequence emphasises a particular person and space: Gilbert (Meylan) steps out of the shadows on a construction dock dressed in worker blues, wearing a mask that he flips back so that he can light a cigarette with his welding iron. His hair is long, his face unshaven. Passionate strains of Vivaldi's 'Summer', a piece that appears throughout Guédiguian's career, play over the images. Cuts move in closer, eventually to a bust shot as he looks up, light brightening his face. He walks up the exterior stairs, again into the light. He has just finished work on his two-week contract and now hops on a bus, conspicuously marked with its destination, L'Estaque-Riaux. In some ways, Guédiguian's entire cinema flows out of this image of a thoughtful young worker, embodied by Meylan, born to the screen, dreaming of a bigger world but firmly attached to and bathed in the luminosity of his space.

Guédiguian has claimed that he 'wrote the story of Gilbert and some "raggazi" while thinking of the social state of his neighbourhood and Pier Paolo Pasolini' (Danel 2008: 45). Pasolini's influence is literary as much as cinematic since it comes here mainly from Pasolini's pre-film-career novel, *Una vita violenta* (*A Violent Life*, 1968). *Dernier été* bears the trace of this influence in at least two ways, the first of which (we will return to the second further on) concerns characters (the raggazi) and thematic development. Pasolini's novel recounts the story of Tomasso, a street kid from the outskirts of Rome, who does what he can to survive on the streets, plotting inventive thefts or turning tricks. Though he seems completely amoral, Tomasso has a growing ethical conscience and a close relationship to his friends, a slapdash gang of 'smartasses' with picturesque names ('Shitter', Zucabbo and Zimmìo). Friendships eventually grow into a code of moral behaviour that is no less real for being outside most ethical codes. Friendships deepen: later in a tuberculosis sanatorium, he befriends Gugliemi, a sick communist activist, and helps him hide from the police during a revolt of hospital workers. After his release, Tomasso even considers joining the party but finds the leaders corrupt. He dedicates himself to his friends and fiancée, until a flood devastates the old shanty town where he grew up: in an act of extreme courage he wades through the treacherous waters to save a few of the inhabitants, but this aggravates his tuberculosis and he dies. Friendship transforms Tomasso from hood into tragic hero.

Dernier été represents similar characters in similar situations: Gilbert (a portmanteau name combining the first names of Meylan and Guédiguian and usually shortened to 'Bert') and his friends, Mario (Jean-Pierre Moreno), Le Muet (Hamzaoui) and Banane (Djamal Bouanane), all in their early twenties, straddle the border between work and delinquency. They share with Pasolini's characters the slangy names and their anti-social masculine bravado. They spend most of their time drinking, talking and playing table football in cafés.

One might mistake their relationship for a superficial pleasure friendship. But a more complex relationship emerges in the film, especially through the characters' conversations, which go beyond 'smartass' taunting. They make fun, but they also try out their opinions, exploring ethical points of view and developing trust and confidence, bonding into a stronger group. This happens especially through conversation. In one scene, the friends are playing table football when Mario brings up his dilemma: whether to continue to work as a truck driver or to take a job closer to his family in the Lafarge cement factory. He likes driving because it brings him to faraway places (Belgium, Germany, Spain) whereas the other friends have never been anywhere. But Gilbert points out that around the table there is an Italian, a Spaniard and an Arab, and that he doesn't need to leave L'Estaque to see the world. This conversation helps Mario think through his decision, but it also introduces a global/local theme that valorises L'Estaque itself. (This theme will be picked up again in *Marius et Jeannette*.)[2]

Another scene shows how this conversation can become more critical, in the sense of Montaigne's *de la conférence*, and can lead people to revise their evaluative outlooks on social or moral issues. This time the friends are gathered on the café terrace. The camera is fixed on them, at their level, its frame determined by the group of friends while slightly theatrical, in a long duration shot. Michou, a

---

2 In this way, the film responds in the opposite way to Pagnol's *Marius*, in which the old port is generally shot as homogenous and provincial.

gay friend from the neighbourhood, arrives from off-screen. Gilbert asks him why he looks glum, and he explains that his boyfriend has left him. He leaves, and the thick-headed Banane mentions a television programme on the 'problem' of homosexuality in the cinema and art worlds. Gilbert takes Michou's defence, but Banane has no problem with Michou (he's a 'different case', he says) even if he doesn't like 'fags' (*les pédés*) generally. Gilbert replies (many of Guédiguian's scenes are *mises en scène* of this type of back and forth) that Banane speaks that way but has no trouble opening his wallet for gay friends when it comes to having a beer. The camera remains fixed on the group, with Le Muet ('The Mute', who understands everything without speaking) nodding between the two, and the dim Banane reflecting. Though there is no revelation here, the conversation is making him rethink cultural images and his own prejudices through a critical lens.

Guédiguian's friendships do not map evenly onto other close relationships, such as the family, which, as Aristotle pointed out, is not based on free choice and mutual passion. Often family members feel comparison and competition, as is the case with Gilbert's relationship with his brother, Boule. Here that competition involves two vastly opposed attitudes towards the community. Early in the film, Boule has robbed a bar owned by an acquaintance of the family. Though Gilbert and his friends also steal, Boule is becoming a gang leader who steals from friends. Early on, Mario and Gilbert teach Boule and his thuggish partner a lesson by giving them a lift in Mario's truck but then raising the truck bed so that the two have to hold on for dear life or be dumped on the road. Boule may be family, but he has a functional view of others and is thus not a friend. Their rivalry crosses into sentimental territory. At a dance, Boule moves in on Josiane (Ascaride), the girl Gilbert is falling in love with, and when she refuses to kiss him he slaps her. In the ensuing fight with Gilbert, he pulls a knife before Gilbert's friends break up the fight.

This is the first but not the last time Guédiguian gives explicit preference to friends over family. Guédiguian presents the fight through the prism of Gilbert and Mario's friendship. The two sneak Mario out from his family home, hop in Mario's truck and drive off quietly to the dance. They enter a courtyard filled with pop music and dancers from their age down to children. They move through the crowd and stand together, to the side, until they see Josiane and Martine, her friend, who interests Mario. After Boule's attack, Mario and Gilbert return to the truck, where a conversation about Josiane and Martine arises, and they discuss various matters, especially Mario's restlessness, which is threatening his marriage. Friendship bestows layers of meaning on this truck: first, as we have seen, it served as the means by which the friends teach Boule a lesson, and now it is the space of their conversation, its windshield framing the pair, marking their difference and separateness, their concern for each other, their attempts to confront the challenges of life in L'Estaque. Guédiguian also uses self-conscious cinematic techniques to underline friendship, as when they steal a boat for fishing in the bay, and, with the sun glimmering on the waves, a soft iris closes around them.

But social and economic conditions threaten Gilbert's friendships. The simple football table becomes a metonymic expression of their lives. In one long take, five of the friends are filmed around the table in medium long shot, the camera at a slight overhead angle. It is dark, so that the windows behind them become part of the dingy wall, flattening the already shallow space around the table. The only action is the flipping of the fake football players, fixed to bars, just as the friends are fixed in their places. Static sequences like this pile up throughout the film without ever adding up to a story: all they seem to do is walk robotically towards the bar, drink and smoke or wait for buses. In one sequence lasting a quarter of the film, the friends waste the night drinking, stealing a car and hassling a number of people, but mostly they drive the car around in circles (especially around one roundabout they can't seem to exit). In one important scene, Guédiguian uses voiceover to express Gilbert's consciousness of the boredom and solitude. Sitting on the terrace after the bar closes, alone, in the dark, and over shots of the empty streets, Gilbert reflects that for the past ten years he has been repeating the same empty gestures and that he wants to leave everything, 'even my friends': Gilbert thus seems to catch a glimpse at a good life but knows some other forces are at play in the quarter, forces dividing the space in a way that blocks him from a productive life. He admits, 'This life is not his.' This is not a 'coming of age' film in which a character accedes into adulthood, for here there is no life to move on to: 'il est mort ce quartier, et nous avec', says Gilbert before walking out into the dark night.[3]

The film provides a discrete but precise historical explanation for the struggles of this friendship. This is the second trace of Pasolini's influence. A one-shot sequence finds Gilbert's family gathered around the kitchen table eating in front of the television, while offscreen we hear a discussion of Italian society on what sounds like a news interview programme. Philip Anderson has tracked down the source of the speaker's words to a text called 'Genocide' from Pasolini's *Scritti Corsari* and helpfully transcribed the French translation given in the film:

> Je pense, en effet, que la destruction et le remplacement des valeurs dans la société italienne d'aujourd'hui mènent, sans bourreaux ni exécutions de masses, à la suppression de larges portions de la société elle-même. L'Italie vit aujourd'hui, d'une façon dramatique et pour la première fois, le phénomène suivant: de larges strates, qui étaient pour ainsi dire demeurées en dehors de l'histoire – l'histoire de la domination bourgeoise et de la révolution bourgeoise – ont subi un génocide, à savoir cette assimilation au mode et à la qualité de vie de la bourgeoisie.
>
> Mais comment s'effectue ce remplacement de valeurs? Je pense qu'il s'effectue clandestinement, au moyen d'une sorte de persuasion occulte. Alors qu'au temps de Marx c'était la violence explicite, au grand jour, la conquête colonial, l'imposition par la force, aujourd'hui les moyens sont plus subtiles, habiles et complexes, le processus est beaucoup plus techniquement au point et profond. C'est en cachette que les nouvelles valeurs sont substituées aux anciennes, et peut-être ne faut-il pas le dire puisque les grands discours idéologiques sont presque inconnus des masses. La télévision, par exemple ... [4]
>
> (Anderson 2008: 242)

---

[3] 'This neighbourhood is dead, and us with it.'

[4] 'I believe in fact that the destruction and replacement of values in contemporary Italian society lead, without hangmen or mass executions, to the suppression of large strata of society itself. Italy today, dramatically and for the first time, is living through the following phenomenon: large populations, who had, so to speak, remained outside of history (history as a domination of the bourgeoisie, or of the bourgeois revolution) have been subjected to a genocide, to wit, an assimilation to the quality and way of life of the bourgeois.

How does this replacement of values take effect? I think it happens clandestinely, through a kind of occult persuasion. In the time of Marx, it would have

The working class has been 'clandestinely persuaded' to forget the history in which they are marginalised, to slip into a second-rate emulation of the bourgeoisie, and thus disappear from history.[5]

Gilbert's world reflects Pasolini's understanding of the historical moment. At the same time, the *mise en scène*, highly ironic given that this text comes via the working-class family's television (the very means of the class genocide), conveys the tension at the centre of Guédiguian's work. The smug man on the television may give the right diagnosis, but Gilbert talks loudly over the television and boorishly scoops spaghetti out of a pan with his fingers. In later scenes he will insult his father's respect for work and slap his sister who does nothing but apply make-up and listen to the radio. Here he stomps out of the room, while another iris closes in on the table, reminding us that there is unfinished business despite the announcement of an 'end of history'. Gilbert's revolt is two-sided: against an economic system eradicating his class, and also against the passive acceptance of 'genocide'.

The disappearance of a social milieu sabotages the love between Gilbert and Josiane. Before considering this, however, we should not oversell the film as a love story, as it might at first appear. Though the camera, from Gilbert's point of view, eroticises Josiane's body, especially during the dance sequence, Guédiguian avoids drawing a strict division between love and friendship. Ascaride does not conform to typical standards of beauty or sex appeal: her diminutive size, her short hair and her chatty gregariousness all make her effective at playing roles in which *eros* and *philia* meet. They quickly enter into the deep type of conversations that Gilbert has with his other friends. This can be seen in an important scene in which the couple set off in a borrowed car to visit one of the beautiful 'criques', the small inlets

happened through explicit violence: the colonial conquest, the imposition of power; whereas today the means are subtler, cleverer, and more complex; the process is technically deeper and more refined. The new values are substituted for the old ones in an invisible manner, and perhaps we should not even mention it, since grand ideological discourses are almost unknown to the masses. Television for example...'.

5 Anderson argues that this inserted text might be read as a 'pretext to define a position from which the viewer can interpret the film and indeed the world that Guédiguian projects', and it is true that the end, or 'genocide' of the working class looms over Guédiguian's work as a continual threat (Anderson 2008: 242).

that dot the coast above Marseilles. (It is the first of the innumerable important car scenes in Guédiguian's cinema.) They shyly talk about dancing but move on to employment and the difficulties they will have in realising aspirations to skilled jobs that seem remote and unattainable: Josiane would like to design dresses; Gilbert would like to create wrought-iron doors.

A close analysis of this sequence shows how deeply their budding *philia* is linked to space and history. The couple drives under the Viaduct of Méjean (its first of numerous appearances in Guédiguian's work): tall, arching and made of masonry, the railway bridge has a timeless look to it. Along with the cement works (which makes its first of many appearances in Guédiguian's work) and the various views of L'Estaque and surrounding areas, the viaduct calls to mind the paintings of L'Estaque by artists such as Georges Braque, or, most of all, Paul Cézanne, who first visited the region with Émile Zola. One of Cézanne's most famous paintings depicts L'Estaque in a well-ordered composition, devoid of human bodies, with geometrical and shimmering shapes of the red roofs, the clay walls and chimneys, standing in chromatic balance with a deep blue bay. Analysing it, Meyer Schapiro refers to Cézanne's 'favoured high view' from above the town and adds that 'a marvellous peace and strength emanate from this work – the true feeling of the Mediterranean, the joy of an ancient nature which man has known how to sustain through the simplicity of his own constructions' (2004: 74). Guédiguian's film turns this image of L'Estaque upside down, creating new images on a human scale and from a human point of view, as if the perspective had fallen from the heights of the cliffs to inside the town's life. In this scene, the point of view is again a fixed camera, this time inside the car, observing the characters within the confines of their world, lacking a larger purview while simultaneously careening around corners and passing perilously close to the cliffs. The camera plunges forward without really moving, stuck in this car, with the rock and blue sea appearing on the other side of the windshield: harmony is replaced with wild movement.

Here and in other films, Guédiguian's characters have an ambiguous relation to nature, and especially the sea. Two examples demonstrate how harmony with nature is reimagined according to the characters' relations. The first is archetypical of how Guédiguian films Meylan. Gilbert arrives at the beach and immediately becomes the centre of the other characters' gazes. He strips to his swimming costume and takes position on top of an old sand-loading machine situated at the top of a cliff, another sign of L'Estaque's economic past. His is filmed from afar, backlit in profile in the hazy sun, as he executes a perfectly balanced and elegant swan dive. Here the film shows him in a gorgeous luminosity, in the Mediterranean sun, but also lit up with love and friendship.[6] The second stand-out moment comes when the couple arrives at the *crique*. Outside of the car, the wind blows through the sparse vegetation, sending a play of light and shadow moving around them. Josiane's rose-coloured dress, slightly transparent and billowing to show her body, echoes Cézanne's colours. As they descend into the crique, they are again a part of nature, though there are signs of detritus, a tyre and a few pieces of rubbish. They are oblivious to the boat in the harbour as they kiss passionately on the beach. The camera cuts closer, eventually to a close-up of their faces as they kiss entirely alone. The fade to black comes consciously but non-ironically from romantic cinema: they are together in a way the viewer cannot follow. This is an iconic scene for Guédiguian, one that will be recycled in *La Ville est tranquille*, as a flashback towards a radiant past moment.

These perfect moments, however, receive a cruel response in the next shot. During the fade-out we are discreetly moved into Gilbert's dark bedroom, where a sudden, blinding light pours out of the screen as he opens the shutters the next morning. A new frame (the window) has opened up, this one vertical and too small to contain the image of the immense factory that faces Gilbert's room. The building lacks both the chromatic harmony of Cézanne's painting (the factory is a bleached grey) and the scale (it literally expands out of the frame in every direction). Standing in the dark bedroom, shown from behind, the space flattened by the darkness and the entering light, Gilbert, nearly naked in his red underwear (the only pleasant colour), appears vulnerable and dominated. A cut shows the factory from outside, again with no human presence; another shows more factories, their chimneys pumping out smoke; another view, darker with a grey sky; another cut to two more rows of buildings, identical,

---

6 One critic has argued that the sea functions in Guédiguian's work something like an amniotic liquid, shaping the human lives of those who live near it (McGonagle 2007: 238).

repetitive, oppressive. On the soundtrack we hear the low buzz of factory machinery. A passenger train catches his attention, suggesting potential escape, and the scene ends.

Dernier été portrays a handsome young man from L'Estaque in 1980, a friend and a lover, stuck in the endgame of his history. The film ends brusquely when Gilbert allows Banane to take him along to steal some money from an old man who hoards cash in an armoire. He also has a gun, and, as the boys run off with the money, he shoots Gilbert fatally in the back.[7] But Guédiguian's *mise en scène* and editing concentrate on the effects of Gilbert's death on the group, which now has lost its glue. It ends on a number of soon-to-be reactions to Gilbert's disappearance, all linked through the mourning sadness of Vivaldi's *Nisi Dominus*: Banane's confused eyes stare blankly as Gilbert dies in his arms; Josiane waits in vain for Gilbert to pick her up; Boule, having perhaps learned something after all, apologises to her and Mario when he passes them on the street. The final images point beyond this particular group to indicate an entire generation: first a kid teases an even younger boy who asks him for a cigarette and then a last shot shows children in long shot, playing soccer on an abandoned lot dominated by surrounding rocky hills. Gilbert's death, and a diminished *philia*, will leave others, not only his present friends but also future groups of kids, less prepared to face the future.

Rouge midi (1983)

Rouge midi begins with a character very similar to Gilbert: Sauveur (Meylan), scruffy but dressed in a nice jacket, looking out over L'Estaque at daybreak. A long shot freezes the sun as it breaks over the mountains: we are at a moment of change and transition, between yesterday and today, and Sauveur is smoking the first cigarette of what will be an important day. A voiceover again indicates solitude. Past and present merge: 'Je les vois sans âge. Le temps n'est pas passé sur eux,

---

7 The film may be evoking here the atmosphere of '*auto-justice*' or vigilantism that spiked in the early 1980s just after the abolition of the death penalty: this man takes Gilbert's life for a small pile of cash. (See the 1982 vigilante film *Légitime défense* [Serge Leroy] for an exploitative cinematic example.)

c'est eux qui sont passés. Je les vois droits, fiers et gais, doués d'une absolue vitalité : J'ai trop de mémoire.'[8] There follows a fade to black and then a busy narrative fresco showing four generations of one family in flashback, unfolding in what Guédiguian has likened to a series of 'tableaux successifs' or a book of images, through which the history of Guédiguian's L'Estaque is told (Derobert and Goudet 1997: 43). The film thus provides this prototypical character with a genealogy, opening a perspective on the history of industrialisation in L'Estaque, culminating in a liminal moment rather than a realisation of promise.

The first tableau begins with the arrival of Sauveur's great-grandparents as immigrants from Italy at the train station of Riaux and their settlement in L'Estaque, sometime near the beginning of the century. The film shows this as a period of mythical hardship and toughness as these peasants with their thick accents attempt to adapt their lives to the promises of industrial modernism and a new culture. L'Estaque is still close to its rural origins, similar to Renoir's *Toni* (1935), an important film for Guédiguian, though here the father of the family finds low-paying work on the docks. The patriarch is tall and lean and teaches the two sons, Guido and Salvatore, to be tough and to endure sacrifices.

The film gives more space to this second generation as those who were children when they arrived or were first-generation born in L'Estaque now grown to adulthood. It emphasises not a single family but a community grouped around a centre of Maggiorina and her boyfriend Jérôme and spreading out to her family, friends (Mindou and Ginette) and a number of local characters. One of the closest relationships is between Jérôme and Mindou, his inseparable friend since childhood. In some ways they are an odd couple: Jérôme does hard legitimate work whereas Mindou is covered in tattoos, becomes a pimp and teases Jérôme for working. The two evoke the history of L'Estaque, competing in childhood swimming contests and, later, the L'Estaque tradition of the *joutes provençales*, most of which were won by Jérôme, just as he also wins the hand of Maggiorina while Mindou silently pines for her. Despite this, they are profoundly committed to each other.

---

8 'I see them ageless ... time hasn't passed over them; they have passed away. I see them upright, proud and gay, endowed with an absolute vitality. I have too much memory.'

Working outward from these friendships, the film undoes two types of popular cinematic images. The first is the gangster film, a common representation of 1930s Marseilles, such as the buddy vehicle *Borsalino* (1970) and its sequel, *Borsalino & Cie* (1974), in which Alain Delon and Jean-Paul Belmondo play roles superficially similar to Jérôme and Mindou. The macho Mindou even wears the Borsalino hat that gave the franchise its title. But if *Borsalino* appeals to escapism into inter-war sets and costumes (casinos, mansions and scantily clad girls) and revels in mafia violence, Guédiguian's film de-emphasises crime and replaces the mafia subtext with the political history of the 1930s and 1940s: Jérôme organises a group of workers, including Maggiorina's brothers, to humiliate fascist poster-hangers and strike; Guido dies on the job as an underwater construction worker due to faulty equipment (building the tunnel of the Rove, still to be seen in L'Estaque); even Mindou leaves town rather than run guns for fascists in Spain. The film also avoids representing large-scale historical events. (There is also a missing Resistance film here.) Instead, action originates in ordinary domestic or common spaces and everyday conversations. Social forces are traced in their impact on everyday life and are set in work spaces: the mounds of sand where the men vote for strikes or the mansion where Maggiorina must put up with the antics of the factory owners.

Concentrating on domestic spaces opens a perspective on the gendered experience of political struggles. Though Ginette is abused by Mindou (one of the film's sympathetic characters) and becomes a prostitute, she is not relegated to the status of object, of sexual desire or violent tendencies, as are the women in films such as *Borsalino*. Instead, the viewer empathises with her suffering as a prostitute and in her complicated relationship with Mindou. We get to know her personal world: her room becomes familiar to us, and we remain with her, even as the other characters forget her, as she advances into extreme old age. For her part, Maggiorina undermines stereotypes of the stay-at-home mother: at one point she is fed up with cooking and bathing kids and demands to come along to the strike; later, she works while Jérôme, after the war, cannot find a job. Class creates power roles that affect both genders: having taken a job as a chauffeur, Jérôme must endure the advances of the sex-crazed sister of the cement-factory owner. Generally, and despite its admiration for the historical struggle of its characters, the film condemns the patriarchy and machismo of the period, shown in Mindou's relationship to Ginette, or through the hairdresser who has helped Maggiorina's parents arrive in L'Estaque and believes he is entitled to her hand in marriage. (Later, he tries to rape her.) In general, women are constrained and oppressed, but they are aware and resistant.

The third tableau picks up similar themes in their evolution into the 1950s, while focusing on Jérôme and Maggiorina's son, Pierre, now a young schoolteacher. Pierre adds to class struggle an intellectual dimension that was never expressed in his parents' generation: when Mindou quotes a phrase read in the newspaper, he recognises Marcus Aurelius; he lends *Les Misérables* to one of his pupils; he also agrees with the utopian idealism he reads in William Morris's *News from Nowhere*, whose money-free and happy society he likens to a post-revolution society. Lying nude in the grass with his girlfriend while reading (the male nude, rather than the female, is foregrounded here), Pierre also reflects more egalitarian attitudes towards sexuality.

Pierre is also an organiser for the Communist Party, though his organising demonstrates some of Guédiguian's ambivalence with regards to communism. Pierre's uncle, Salvatore, exemplifies the militant tradition, but he is killed on the steps of the Marseilles Opera during a demonstration. The next day Pierre enters a bar full of workers, steps onto his soapbox and tries, in the name of the party, to invite the men to rally in support of their fallen comrade. Nobody seems to be listening, and one worker shouts rudely at him, 'Tu casses les couilles.'[9] But then another of the other workers throws down his last card, walks to the man at the bar and drags him out by his collar. He tells Pierre to continue, and Pierre now invites them to a silent march without flags or political tracts. The men are convinced in advance: resistant to appropriation for party ends but in complete solidarity with their fallen friend. This de-affiliation of political solidarity, reflecting Guédiguian's own departure from the party, will be a growing theme in his cinema. (See my discussion at the beginning of Chapter 3.)

Named to honour Salvatore, Sauveur is linked to the first generation, to the past and to the anti-fascist and workers' struggle. Three generations meet at his first communion (which he dreads, in an

9 'You're pissing me off.'

anti-clerical nod). But Jérôme, with whom the young Sauveur has a close relationship, observes through him a breakdown in continuity: 'Sauveur ne vivra pas comme nous.'[10] Sauveur even witnesses the death of that generation: he is playing on a scrap heap when his father comes to announce his grandfather's death, and it is Sauveur who must break the news to Maggiorina. In this way, the film suggests a break: how will Sauveur's life continue at this liminal stage in history?

The film thus cuts ahead to its final tableau, a day or two preceding Sauveur's departure. This shorter sequence has a destabilised feel, due to the accumulation, now for the third or fourth time, of settings from earlier tableaux, and thus layers of history. We have seen Jérôme and Mindou swim in front of the Prud'homie de Pêche building and then Pierre catching shellfish in front of the same building. We have observed Jérôme and Maggiorina in their apartment, the same apartment, newly painted, where the elderly Maggiorina receives the news of Jérôme's death. We have seen the café, restored by Mindou, where he displays the statue of the virgin that has been present throughout the entire film. In this last sequence, Sauveur spends his last day and night wandering through these spaces with friends. They walk through the church square and decide to have a pee. Sauveur observes that a passing ship looks like 'a village', but what he cannot know is that Salvatore had made exactly the same observation when he was a child. A watchman with two German shepherds patrols the Prud'homie de Pêche and the port. A montage of shots– the café, the barbershop, the jousting boats and others, all unoccupied or unused – marks the transition back to Sauveur, sitting alone on the balcony as in the first shot of the film, filled with memories from which he is cut off.

When Sauveur sets out the next day, the direction he is taking is not at all clear. His best friend Malek (Hamzaoui) drops him at the Saint-Charles SNCF station in Marseilles. ('Le Muet' of *Dernier été* pronounces only one word before choking up – 'Ciao!') The final shot is a long and beautiful sweeping view from Sauveur's perspective in the train: it looks backwards at the passing city, the docks, the large ships, then down on L'Estaque, ships in harbour, then the famed viaduct, the countryside, the rocky and green hills of the mountains,

10 'Sauveur will not live as we have lived.'

before entering the tunnel where everything goes black. A bit like Walter Benjamin's angel of history, he is being sucked into an uncertain future while contemplating the fragmented past, detached from the History towards which it was supposed to lead. He is now displaced, lacking a home and community.

In *Rouge midi*, Guédiguian begins a lifelong experimentation in the use of actors. Given such a sprawling narrative, a big budget filmmaker would perhaps take pride in making the succession of generations as believable as possible, by either choosing different actors to represent characters at different stages of life or employing talented make-up artists. But as we move from Maggiorina, Jérôme and Mindou as young adults to their middle and old ages, Guédiguian barely makes any effort at changing his actors' appearance: the grey of Meylan's hair looks sprayed on; the elderly Maggiorina has the clear gaze and wrinkle-free face that she had as a young woman. Critics at the time were judging by realist standards when they giggled through the film's screening at Cannes, in a cruelly embarrassing episode for Guédiguian and his actors and the beginning of a sometimes-strained relationship with critics. And it is true that the effect can be awkward, such as when Jérôme embraces his mother (another Guédiguian regular, Frédérique Bonnal), who, despite the make-up and fake grey, doesn't appear a day older than he does.

And yet, one can also interpret the use of actors as an initial attempt at what will be some of Guédiguian's most original cinematic explorations, inspired by Brecht's 'short organum' and the theory of the 'alienation effect'. An A-effect results, for instance, when Meylan plays, quite obviously, characters from separate periods in time, or when he himself appears on screen with actors his age, barely disguised, playing much older characters. This turns the body into a place where the viewer can perceive successive periods of history. It also carves out a distance between the actor and the role he or she is playing. As Brecht argues, 'at no moment must he [the actor] go so far as to be wholly transformed into the character played' (1992: 193). By retaining his or her thoughts and emotions while playing a role, the actor invites the audience to reflect as well: the action is thereby historicised, shown in its 'impermanence', with the suggestion that things could possibly be ushered in another direction (Brecht 1992: 190). In *Rouge midi*, the viewer is conscious that these stories are not destinies but products of a group of actors exploring the meaning of the past and its implications for an unknown future. At the same time, the film's ending does not yet suggest that they see a way forward in Sauveur's historical moment.

Ki lo sa? (1985)

Guédiguian's following film, *Ki lo sa?* leaves behind the ambitious perspective and multigenerational fresco of *Rouge midi* to focus tightly on a small group of four friends in the immediate present. The film is also less anchored in daily life and realism than *Dernier été*. It in fact takes place to the side of society. It begins, in its very first scene, by introducing Jean-Pierre Darroussin to Guédiguian's cinema. We are in the park of a stately house, where Dada (using Darroussin's real-life nickname), sits next to a water basin surrounded by flowers he has just planted, reading a letter. The son of the cook and the gardener who have now died, Dada cares for the grounds of the home, which has been more or less abandoned by its owners. They, however, have decided to return, and he will have to move out. Dada is a naïve, sensitive, indecisive character, who will not be able to find any other kind of work. The film cuts back and forth between Dada and three other characters, his friends, who are at present alone and alienated like him. A cut from the garden brings us to a dilapidated apartment building squatted by Gitan (Meylan). Framed by a shaky, handheld camera, he gets up, rinses with booze and heads off into the city to panhandle until evening, though he sleeps most of the day. After a quick cut back to Darroussin, we turn to Marie (Ascaride), aka Charlot, meeting a man (Alain Lenglet) in the port: she is probably a prostitute, though this is unstated. Another quick cut to Darroussin and then to Pierrot's house, actually his parents', where he still lives, struggling to make his way as a writer. Pierrot (Pierre Banderet) seems to have serious artistic pretensions, wracking his brain for the next line. But his work is only a crass and exploitative pornographic novel: he reads out loud as he writes: 'She took his member into her mouth.' We later find out that these characters are frustrated idealists: Gitan is a former political organiser and anarchist; Charlot a history student interested in the labour movement; and Pierrot a literary writer. But they have either become completely marginal (Gitan) or instruments of a vulgar sexual exploitation (Charlot and Pierrot). The sequence finally cuts back to Dada, who says, staring at his reflection in the fountain, that 'they will all come'; and, almost magically, they do: first Marie, then Gitan who hesitates at the gate and finally Pierrot.

The garden is propitious for a meeting between these former friends and adds an almost abstract quality to the consideration of friendship. The film insists on beauty of the space (though it is somewhat overgrown): with its handsome trees and flowers and sheltered alleys, the walled-in garden is reminiscent of the medieval garden or the *locus amoenus* studied by Ernst Robert Curtius (see Curtius 2013: 192). Such a space, and Dada's childlike character, might also call to mind Ernst Bloch's discussion of the 'hiding place' (Bloch 1995: 22). For Bloch, hiding places in fairy tales, daydreams and children's games are places we can indulge in utopian thoughts: 'We seek out a corner, it protects and conceals ... Our own room is prefigured here, the free life that is coming' (Bloch 1995: 22). They enter a utopian hiding space.

There is only a hint at the longer history of the friendship. Disembodied voices of children float on the soundtrack as the three arrive, suggesting a childhood connection, and we find out later that they had made a pact, ten years ago, to return to this site of their childhood games on this date. Moreover, there are ambiguous shots of children in the film. Their clothes do not fit into an obvious time period, and one of the children resembles Gitan, so at times these scenes feel like flashbacks, but at other times they seem like different kids, in the present, separated from the friends by the garden wall and invading the courtyard when they are away. The oneiric anti-realism is intentional: the past surrounds them in the present, and the present seems to imply repetition across generations. These children represent an age of enjoyment, without parents or other adults, filled with running in the street, games of soccer and general anarchical play. There is an implied narrative of friendship here: one can imagine these friendships maturing more deeply into young adulthood. In the case of the four principal characters, however, that period is skipped, and we find them in their late twenties or early thirties, where they have the task of renewing the story that began so many years ago.

Guédiguian even includes in the film a standard by which they can measure their friendship, in the form of a letter read to the others by

Pierrot, who has been writing in a private nook of the garden. I will return to the *mise en scène* of this instance of writing, but in reality the passage comes from a letter written by the poet René Char to his friend, André Breton. Its contents sum up the particular values of friendship for Guédiguian and are relevant for all his films:

> Où en suis-je aujourd'hui? Je ne sais au juste. J'ai de la difficulté à me reconnaître sur le fil des évidences dont je suis l'interné et le témoin. Ce n'est pas moi qui ai simplifié les choses, mais les choses horribles m'ont rendu simple, plus apte à faire confiance à certains au fond desquels subsistent, tenaces, les feux mourants de la recherche et de la dignité humaine, ailleurs déjà anéantis et balayés, méprisés et niés. C'est vous dire que si certains prodiges ont cessé d'exister pour moi, je n'en défends pas moins, de toute mon énergie, le droit de s'affirmer prodigieux. Je ne serai jamais assez perdu dans mon indépendance ou son illusion, pour avoir le cœur de ne plus aimer les fortes têtes désobéissantes qui descendent au fond du cratère, sans se soucier des appels du bord. Ce juron, quand je parle de l'espoir, c'est un bien que je ne possède plus, mais il me plait qu'il existe chez d'autres. Rien de banal entre nous. Nous avons su et nous saurons nous retrouver à la seconde excessive de l'essentiel. Notre particularité consiste à n'être indésirables qu'en fonction de notre refus de signer le dernier feuillet, celui de l'apaisement: celui-ci s'arrache ou nous est enlevé.[11]

Ki lo sa? is the first of a sub-genre of films that will recur in Guédiguian's career, and which he refers to as the *film bilan* or the 'stocktaking' film. Has friendship allowed us to grow as humans, or to push society in a better direction? Char's letter similarly takes stock

[11] 'Where do I stand today? I don't know exactly. I have trouble recognising myself on the string of foregone conclusions to which I am both prisoner and witness. It is not I who have simplified things, but those horrid things that have left me simple, and more willing to give confidence to those few whose tenacious hearts still fan the waning embers of quest and human dignity, elsewhere reduced to dust and swept away, disdained and denied. What I mean to say is that if some wonders have ceased to exist for me, I do not defend any less, and with all my energy, the right to claim oneself wondrous. I will never be so lost in my independence, or its illusion, that I no longer love the hard-headed and disobedient, those who climb to the bottom of the crater and pay no heed to the calls from the rim. That cry, when I speak of hope, is a good I no longer possess, but it pleases me that it exists for others. Nothing banal between us. We have found, and will continue to find each other at the excessive moment of the essential. Our particularity consists in being undesirables only in so far as we refuse to sign the last page, the page of consent: this can only be torn away or stolen from us.'

of the world and his relationship with close friends. Guédiguian's characters, living in an alienated and banal present, reflect Char's imprisonment on a 'string of foregone conclusions' and in 'simple' lives, filled with boredom and empty 'pleasures'. Char's friendship with Breton offers hope in the 'dying embers' of 'searching and human dignity', something like what our four characters are seeking in this garden. The 'excessive moment of the essential' puts meaningfulness, the essential, in dialogue with difference, or 'going beyond'. Friendship gives 'hope' (a new relation to the future), but one must resist capitulation for the world (the 'horrible things') exerts much pressure to renounce these other types of relation.

With their backgrounds – Marie a student of socialism, Pierrot a writer, Gitan an anarchist, one of Char's 'hard-headed' – these friends should be willing to leave the beaten path to seek change and resistance. But their present lives prove that they are very far from Char's ideal. They cannot even manage to restore the garden to its former beauty: years of alcoholism have made Gitan too tired; Pierrot is too busy lusting over Charlot; Dada too depressed. When they attempt to reconstruct their past relationship, by chasing each other around the alleys or pushing each other in the fountain, they come off as puerile and self-conscious, aping the kids' games. Char's letter itself is presented with acute irony: Pierrot has been struggling to write something creative and new, but he presents Char's writing as his own in a dramatic reading, and Gitan call him on the plagiarism. They all wind up fighting: Pierrot attacks Gitan, the alcoholic, who calls Dada a simpleton and Marie a prostitute. Rather than Char's 'tenacious hearts', Gitan admits that 'nous sommes des inadaptés'.[12] If Char still refuses to sign the 'last page of consent', the 'bilan' of this film suggests that it is too late: they have given up and are no longer prodigious.

Ki lo sa? is stylistically more self-conscious and bitterly ironic, not only in terms of its setting and its artificial acting style but also in its use of music. The disjunction between the friends' former selves and their present reality is reflected in a non-diegetic music (a rarity in Guédiguian's cinema) written by then first-time and now well-known film composer Alexandre Desplat. Flutes, woodwinds and warm strings are coupled with an edgier dulcimer, all of which add

12 'We are maladjusted.'

to the separate and abstract quality of the semi-utopian space of the gardens. The music is at times joyous and childish but at other times serious or lyrical; but most often it is in an ironic relation to the characters, cheery when they are the most depressed, with a sincere emotionality that has trouble matching up with their bad faith. Guédiguian's use of popular music, more typical of his cinema as a whole, suggests a more collective despondency. In one long scene, the friends drive to the Calanque du Grand Méjean for a swim; on the radio, Bob Dylan's 1966 'I Want You' evokes the freedom of the open road and emotional investments of its period, but the friends' discussion turns rapidly into reminders of their failure. Dylan's presence seems to imply the failure not just of these friends but also of a whole generation of formerly idealistic youth who have given up on their dreams and desires by the mid-1980s.

Rather than letting them return to their solitary lives or remain wallowing in their failed friendship, Dada, with Gitan's complicity, decides to spike their last cup of coffee with poison. This hopeless conclusion is only partially redeemed when, in a Brechtian move, the film comments on itself: in the closing scene, the children break into the garden, run through the weeds and alleys and play around the cadavers. The younger version of Gitan stares thoughtfully at the dead man. As the camera pans up from the fountain to the blue sky for a final shot, we hear sounds of joy and laughter. Once again these kids may represent their previous selves, or it could be that they represent another generation, reborn despite their failure. *Ki lo sa?* (phonetically, in Italian, 'Who knows?'). The film ends on this dark and bitter comedy. Guédiguian called it a film about 'how to believe in nothing' (Derobert and Goudet 1997: 43).

Dieu vomit les tièdes (1989)

Dieu vomit les tièdes reunites these actors, in nearby Martigues, to form another group of four down-on-their-luck friends, this time with perhaps Guédiguian's most pessimistic view of his historical present. The film was shot during the summer of 1989, in part at the height of the commemoration of the French Revolution, an event crucially incorporated into the storyline. It begins with Cochise (Darroussin), a writer, at a posh literary party in Paris, being pressured by his editor to finish his book on the Revolution, scheduled soon to be adapted into a television series. Cochise is a novel character for Guédiguian in the sense that he has left the neighbourhood and become a successful writer, dealing with a theme that concerns the entire nation and that will be broadcast to a wide audience. But things are not going well for Cochise, who is drunk and suffering and who replies that neither he nor anyone else 'gives a shit' ('on s'en bat les couilles') about the Revolution; in fact, he asserts that he, Cochise, *is* the Revolution, and that the editor simply wants him to 'bury' it, and thus himself. That night he gives up on his book and return to Martigues.

Dieu vomit les tièdes thereby enters a furious contemporary debate about the legacy of the French Revolution and its relation to communism and other militant movements. The debate is too complex to reproduce fully, but François Furet once again plays a leading and very public role in it. According to Furet, the most influential twentieth-century historians of the Revolution, especially Albert Mathiez and Georges Lefebvre, misguided by their Marxist-communist ideology, have transmitted a flawed interpretation of the Revolution as an uprising of the proletariat against capital and a repressive king (Furet and Ozouf 1989: 881–99). Mathiez especially had considered the Bolsheviks, and later the Soviet Union, as the inheritors of the Jacobins; he had also 'loved' Robespierre for his virtue, chastity and inflexibility (Furet and Ozouf 1989: 893). Furet led an unorganised group of revisionist historians contesting this interpretation, claiming a little gloatingly that the analogy between the French and Russian revolutions was now coming back 'like a boomerang' against those who were 'obsessed by the Russian revolution' (Furet and Ozouf 1989: xix).

Furet insisted instead that the Revolution be understood as a top-down reform movement that had veered into mass revolt until moderates in the Third Republic successfully redrew a distinction between deliberative democracy and violent revolution. Democracy, in his view, was not something to be seized by the proletariat, but to be inched towards slowly. Furet writes, with Mona Ozouf, that changes in France since 1950 largely indicated that the Revolution had successfully run its course:

> There are no longer many peasants, and the middle class is much larger than it was. The exile of our working class, to which the

Communist Party lent dignity, is ending before our eyes. The society is more modern, and the French people are much more similar to one another than they were a century ago. As a result, however, they have less need of the unity that teachers once tried to foster by keeping memories of the Revolution alive. Absorbed into a common culture, less dependent than in the past on outspoken and militant loyalties, the republican memory is fading as a consequence of its own success.

(Furet and Ozouf 1989: xx)

Though Furet admits to a few stubborn 'enemies capable of being roused to action', he seems to be endorsing once again a version of the 'end of history' thesis, in the spirit of which Cochise has been asked to write his screenplay for the television: thus people 'don't give a shit' about the Revolution (i.e. they have been 'assimilated' or depoliticised), and the editor is trying to 'bury' him, for he refuses to let go of it. For an example of what Cochise is talking about one could point to Robert Enrico and Richard Heffron's thoroughly neutral and academic 1989 blockbuster, *La Révolution française*, on which the historian Jean Tulard, an admirer of Furet, served as historical consultant.

Cochise is anything but neutral with regards to the Revolution. Early scenes link Cochise with his childhood friends in L'Estaque and Martigues: Frisé (Meylan), a tough long-haired marginal who lives in a little shack and paints, over and over, image of the Caronte viaduct; Tirelire (Ascaride), a waitress at a tea room, who sleeps around and sings karaoke to old people; and Quatre Oeil (Banderet), the low-talent editor of a third rate newspaper.[13] Recurring flashbacks bring us to the viaduct in the 1960s. ('US go home' is spray-painted on its central column.) The four friends, as children, sneak into the central column where they sign a pact: 'Nous, fils de pauvres, jurons de nous battre jusqu'à la mort et quoi qu'il arrive pour que vienne un jour où tout le monde sera riche, sans être capitaliste. Si l'un de nous trahissait ce serment, les autres ne lui parleraient plus jamais.'[14] Over

13 The Caronte Viaduct is a unique swinging bridge connecting railway lines over the Caronte channel near Martigues. The iron bridge sits on three steel-reinforced concrete columns built in the channel. To allow ships to pass, the bridge turns on its central tower, which also contains its mechanical workings. Built in 1914, the bridge figures prominently in Jean Renoir's *Toni*, an important film for Guédiguian.

14 'We, sons of the poor, swear to fight until death, no matter what happens, so that the day may come when everyone will be rich without being capitalists. If any of us should betray this pact, the others will never speak to him again.'

Tirelire's objection that women were excluded in the term 'sons', they all sign in their blood.[15] Cochise's revolution takes place far from the national scene, in the companionship of a few friends, and is dedicated to class solidarity. Returning home is a way of attempting to reconstruct this personal revolution.

Guédiguian does not share Furet's optimistic view that the Republic has constructed a basically unified nation: on the ground, in Cochise's neighbourhood, poverty and social division still call for struggle. Unemployment is high: their younger friend Karim must shine shoes for a few francs, and many are forced to borrow money from a usurer. Criminality is high: Karim's brother Rachid is a pimp and drug dealer who sells to the local kids. And racism has become a wedge: the men setting up the Bastille Day 'revolutionary village' belong to a Front National type club that harasses the local Arab population. In this detail, Guédiguian touches upon a critique of the commemoration made by Steven L. Kaplan in his analysis of the bicentenary commemoration: even if Furet primarily wanted to criticise overzealousness, his obsessive focus on anti-communism in part legitimised a nationalist extremism that Kaplan sees in reactionary historians such as Pierre Chaunu. Moreover, 1989 marked the first official participation of the Front National in the Marseilles city elections. Quoting the spirit of some of these historians and political groups, the racists in the film lament the 'moral and cultural decadence' of France, the type of thing that 'leads to the Soviet Union'.

The question is what to do when faced with these problems. When Cochise catches up to his friends, he finds that they too are depressed and have conflicted attitudes towards past commitments. Two of them have adapted through accommodation: Tirelire, the least intelligent of all Guédiguian's women, spends her time sleeping around and serving tea to elderly ladies, while Quatre Oeil, who feels threatened because he is of Serbian origin, meekly follows orders at the newspaper. Far more interesting, however, is Frisé (Meylan), the leader of the group and a complicated and Robespierre-like figure. Frisé has remained radically and virtuously attached to the oath. In town he is

15 They also change the word 'worker' to 'poor', in a first reference to a recurring figure in Guédiguian's cinema, the 'pauvres gens', a purposely vague reference to anyone in an economically oppressed class. See the section on *Les Neiges du Kilimandjaro*, which originally was called *Les Pauvres Gens*.

silent and nervous, but he is more comfortable in the marginal space in which he has built his little shack, next to the viaduct. Here he has two main occupations, both of which are highly idealistic. First, he offers a place to neighbourhood children to gather and helps them in various ways: teaching them ping pong, the violin or putting them to work. One episode throws this activity into turmoil: when one boy drops a syringe from his pocket, Frisé violently throws him out, along with all the other kids, and he finds himself alone again. (Guédiguian underlines this solitude with an iris transition.)

But mainly, in his solitude, Frisé paints, over and over, the same view of the viaduct. The viaduct provides a metonymic connection to working-class history: Jean Renoir semi-famously used it in his film about the trials and tribulations of the new immigrants from Italy, *Toni* (1935). The central column of the viaduct is now spray-painted with a slogan reflecting contemporary divisions – 'les arabes à la mer' ('throw the Arabs into the sea') – but Frisé does not include this in the pristine and pure image he paints. Frisé's willed blindness towards the present is disquieting. Later, he shows his friend another painting, framed in such a way that the old reproduction overlays the bridge precisely, replacing the new with the image of the old: 'I live in a décor; I live in a prison: see how it was before when blue was really blue and green was really green.' Guédiguian's composition of images becomes more sophisticated in this film, perhaps thanks to the beginning of a collaboration with cinematographer Bernard Cavalié. One shot shows the window of the shack, in which we see the decentred reflection of Frisé painting the bridge. We see the bridge itself, painted on his canvas, and its reflection in the window, all with another newer bridge, the highway bridge in the distant background. An impressive shot such as this suggests a closed reality but also the thinness of that reality, and an encroaching outside world. Frisé's space is one of somewhat insanely pure memory: the only other place in which he feels at home is the Church of the Magdalene in Martigues, where he works at restoring the virgin and cleaning the organ and the tombs. He has retreated into his obsession with History.

Cochise's return to his revolutionary roots thus brings him only fleeting satisfaction and mainly frustration: during a night of drinking, the friends set the racists' bicentenary decorations on fire while singing a communist song, 'Prenez Garde!', but they are just blowing off drunken steam.[16] Lacking is a cohesion between people, or, as Thomas (Jacques Boudet), the bar owner, puts it, in the past, 'before we were poor, but we were poor together, like a family; whereas now everyone looks the same and people are ashamed to show if they are poor.' Thomas serves as a link to the past: he continues to run the bar and invites people to his home on the beach for dinner, where he shares his recipe for spaghetti with clams. (In Guédiguian's cinema, social links are often built over the dinner table and by handing down traditional recipes.) He tosses the racists out of the café, throwing their flags after them. But his presence in the film is fleeting: Guédiguian films the speech about poverty and family in a beautiful Mediterranean light as Thomas and Cochise set off on a fishing excursion, but the two are separate from the world, and Thomas observes sadly that the sea is now empty of ships and fishing vessels.

Less nostalgically, the film is punctuated by a number of shots of dead bodies, suggesting that someone is indeed engaged in concrete action. One by one they wash up in the port to the sounds of military fifes, reminding the viewer of the bicentennial festivities: first an anonymous corpse, then the moneylender, then Rachid the pimp, then the leader of the racist group. These murders, which have taken place off-screen, during cuts, are presented in an ambiguous moral light. The other characters of the film, when they are themselves in private spaces, cannot bring themselves to condemn them. (Cochise's mother admits that she is not sad at the moneylender's death.) The narrative strands come to a head on Bastille Day itself. The night before, Karim had stopped by Thomas's house to share a bouillabaisse with the others, but this time he is with the prostitutes that used to work for his brother. An iris circles in as Frisé refuses to share a drink with him, and we, and eventually Cochise, understand that he is the killer. Cochise finds himself in front of a dilemma that mirrors the historical debate. On one side there is a frightening radical terror: Frisé as Robespierre; on the other side there are the empty celebrations of a republican revolution in an unjust world.[17]

16 'Be Warned': the song was written for the Congrès de Tours in 1920, where the predecessor of the French Communist Party was formed.
17 The moral dilemma of political violence will be dealt with differently in a later film, *L'Armée du crime*, where the context of resistance against the Nazi occupation will provide the justification.

The commemoration takes place with Cochise wandering through the town in shock and confusion, crying, alone, off to the side, as the locals pursue their tacky celebrations and generic firework displays. Meanwhile, Karim is found floating in the port. The next day, Cochise has understood what he must do: he takes a revolver and goes to kill Frisé.

The last shots of the film emphasise another important stylistic feature in Guédiguian's work. The space next to the turning viaduct was also to be the setting of a project that Guédiguian was unable to produce, called *Notre-Dame de la Garde*, or *Paroles d'Evangile*, a farce, which he defines as a genre set in a space outside of society, where instinct and body rule the action, in a world where there were 'no values, no love, no friendship, nothing' (Derobert and Goudet 1997: 44). Spatially, *Dieu vomit les tièdes* is indeed peppered with scenes that centre on bodies: drunk, dead, defecating, working, fighting, often grotesque. The film's end is told through the physical relationship of bodies: with the bullet in him, Frisé falls on Cochise, who lands on the ground, under the weight of his friend. He can't push him off, and the film ends with shots of this valueless and purely physical universe: Cochise pinned under Frisé's dead body, Frisé's empty chair, the shack, the canal, accompanied by the church's organ music and Cochise's multiple, visceral cries of despair.

Cochise has thus renounced the virtue interpretation of the Revolution, and along with it communism and the other failed militant movements of the 1960s and 1970s. But he has not found anything to replace it. Without options, he is again at an apocalyptic moment, and the numerous references to religion underscore a sense of the end of time. The film's title is in fact a quote from a well-known passage of the Book of Revelation (3:14–16). The angel tells John to write to the Laodiceans about what the 'Amen' (the 'faithful and true witness') has to say (the tone of the St James version seems appropriate here): 'I know thy works, that thou art neither cold nor hot: I would thou wert cold or hot. So then because thou art lukewarm, and neither cold nor hot, I will spue thee out of my mouth.' Cochise can be neither hot nor cold, seemingly the only two choices, and still believe in his childhood commitments. His wordless cries express this incapacity to move on.

Despite such pessimism, there may have been some consolation for Guédiguian in the fact that this thematic low point was counterbalanced by an ever-strengthening troupe of friends gathering in his work life. The hard-core trio of Meylan, Hamzaoui and Ascaride was joined by Frédérique Bonnal, Pierre Banderet and Jacques Boudet in *Rouge midi*, Darroussin in *Ki lo sa?*, and here Lenglet, Jacques Pieiller and others. Hamzaoui, Sasia and Cavalié were firmly in place behind the scenes. In the credits, one also finds the names of Alain Guesnier, Yvon Davis and Gilles Sandoz (along with Guédiguian) as producers: this is the group that founded Agat Films & Cie, the independent production company that has supported most of Guédiguian's subsequent work.[18] These collaborations bred a much more hopeful narrative world – it could hardly become gloomier – as Guédiguian moved into the 1990s.

References

Anderson, Philip (2008) 'Stories of Violence, Violence of History: The Political Logic of Guédiguian's Cinema from *Dernier été* (1980) to *La Ville est tranquille* (2001)', *The Australian Journal of French Studies*, 45:3, 238–49.

Aristotle (2011) *Nichomachean Ethics*, Chicago, Ill.: University of Chicago Press.

Curtius, Ernst Robert (2013) *European Literature and the Latin Middle Ages*, Princeton, NJ: Princeton University Press.

Bloch, Ernst (1995) *The Principle of Hope*, vol. I, Cambridge, Mass.: MIT Press.

Brecht, Bertolt (1992) 'A Short Organum for the Theatre', *Brecht on Theatre: The Development of an Aesthetic*, trans. John Willet, New York: Hill & Wang, pp. 179–205.

Danel, Isabelle (2008) *Conversation avec Robert Guédiguian*, Paris: Les Carnets de l'Info.

Derobert, Eric and Stéphane Goudet (1997) 'Entretien avec Robert Guédiguian: "Intervenir dans le monde, plutôt que dans l'histoire du cinéma"', *Positif*, 442, 42–8.

Furet, François and Mona Ozouf (eds.) (1989) *A Critical Dictionary of the French Revolution*, Cambridge, Mass.: Harvard University Press.

Kaplan, Steven L. (1995) *Farewell, Revolution: The Historians' Feud, France, 1789/1989*, Ithaca, NY: Cornell University Press.

McGonagle, Joseph (2007) 'The End of an Era: Marseilles at the Millennium in Robert Guédiguian's *La Ville est tranquille* (2001)', *Studies in French Cinema*, 7:3, 231–41.

Mariette, Audrey (2005) 'Ressources et contraintes d'un passé militant: le cas d'un cinéaste "engagé", Robert Guédiguian', in Sylvie Tissot, Christophe

---

18 Guesnier has since left, and Sandoz was thrown out of the collective during a dispute over a production that put the company in financial difficulties, but the personnel and structure of Agat Films & Cie is starting to take form.

Gaubert and Marie-Hélène Lechien (eds.), *Reconversions militantes*, Limoges: Pulim, pp. 201–29.

Morris, William (1993) *News from Nowhere and Other Writings*, London: Penguin.

Pasolini, Pier Paolo (1968) *A Violent Life*, trans. William Weaver, New York: Pantheon Books.

Schapiro, Meyer (2004) *Cézanne*, New York: Harry N. Abrams.

Tissot, Sylvie, Christophe Gaubert, and Marie-Hélène Lechien (eds.) (2006) *Reconversions militantes*, Limoges: Pulim.

3

Crossing every barrier
The decade of the conte de L'Estaque

Over the course of the four films of the 1980s, we witness Guédiguian's growing despair over the vicissitudes of communism and other forms of leftist militancy. But by exploring so deeply the historical impasse, Guédiguian seems to have performed a kind of political exorcism, and his films of the 1990s shift radically in tone. Looking back at the period in 2011, he would still use the word 'communism' to describe his values, but he redefines the term, taking away its capital 'C' and liberating it from both its revolutionary and Soviet heritage:

> Le mot 'communiste', je souffre énormément de le voir toujours rattaché aux expériences extérieures, alors que je trouve qu'il a des racines françaises très importantes, parce que les communes existaient avant la Révolution de 1789, et à mon avis le mot 'communiste' en vient et je pense qu'il a une origine très liée au mouvement ouvrier français.[1]
> (Sahuc 2011: 30)

In a sense, one could argue that in statements such as this Guédiguian concedes the historians' debate over the legacy of the Revolution. Perhaps History has ended. Martin O'Shaughnessy argues that Guédiguian works somewhere in the 'fragments' of grand narratives of the left. But it might be more accurate to say that, after staring at the problem for such a long time, Guédiguian has perceived something

---

[1] 'I suffer greatly when I see the word 'Communism' always associated with external experiences, whereas I consider that it has very important French roots, since communes existed before the Revolution of 1789, and, in my opinion, 'communist' comes from them, and I think that its origin is closely linked to the French workers' movement.'

more positive and focused, which he had hitherto misunderstood: a different type of communism rooted in small-scale groups, communes, local political movements, predating the Revolution and discernible from (if related to) the history of the Communist Party. Perhaps it never was grand narratives, political parties or the idea of a goal in history that interested Guédiguian in the first place. Perhaps it is, rather, politics at a local level, enacted by small groups of friends and neighbours, like the anarcho-syndicalism of Pierre in *Rouge midi*, the conversations of *Dernier été* or the local resistance to the Front National hinted at in *Dieu vomit les tièdes*.

This new view of politics is not an endorsement of more moderate reforms or a renunciation of action:

> une redistribution fiscale qui soit plus sympathique, moins inégalitaire, tout ça c'est bien. Mais alors on dit qu'on est dans ce cadre-là, et si on est dans ce cadre-là il faut se battre comme ça. Je trouve donc que ça change tout, ça change tous les combats. Alors évidemment, je continue à rêver qu'il y a une possibilité de changer de cadre ... C'est là que je dis que 'le songe d'une chose' comme disait Marx, ne peut être que collectif, mais il faut trouver aussi l'espace pour le faire.[2]
>
> (Sahuc 2011: 30)

For Guédiguian, the return of a redefined communism indeed brings new hope for action (where action in the past was futile), but it also requires new thinking, an exploration of spaces of the imagination that might point towards how to act. To a great extent, the films in this second period will turn back to utopia (which has failed in *Ki lo sa?*) and especially *philia*, as ways of imagining action differently, so that History might move forward again. The goal will not be to reject the world as it is but, rather, to extract from daily experience, by means of the imagination, strategies for improving collective life. The positive energy expressed in these films is at times exhilarating, but towards the end of the period, without renouncing the critical

---

2 'A kinder fiscal redistribution, less inequality, that's all fine. But then we admit that we are still in that framework, and if we are in that framework we have to fight in that way. I feel this changes everything; it changes all combats. So obviously I persist in dreaming that it is possible to change frameworks ... and that's where I say that 'the dream of a thing', as Marx said, can only be collective, but you have to find spaces to make this happen.'

importance of utopia and friendship, Guédiguian does seem to recognise and accept their limits.

L'Argent fait le bonheur (1992)

The shift in attitude was also initiated by a practical constraint, at least for the first film of the period. After *Dieu vomit les tièdes*, Jean-Pierre Cottet, an old friend from Aix-en-Provence, who had become a television producer for France 2, proposed to fund Guédiguian's next film, but only if it were a comedy with 'humour, no deaths, and a positive ending' (Danel 2008: 70). To write the film, Guédiguian paired up with Jean-Louis Milesi, to whom he gives credit for much of the screenplay's verve, and who remains Guédiguian's preferred writing partner today. The humorous title of the resulting film, *L'Argent fait le bonheur*, points with confidence to its positive ending. It even begins at its happy ending: a young blond woman dressed in a bridal gown dances with some Arab women in a small, corrugated hangar; she steps outside to a joyous party, filmed from extreme overhead, with Italian pop replacing the North African music, in the courtyard of a housing project where the building is situated; she joins a table of family members. In classic theatrical tradition, the diverse housing block comes together in celebration of a marriage.

We know already during this scene, however, that the community has had problems. A cut brings us to a man standing at the bar, while another man approaches, hands him a pistol, and says, 'Here you are, Father, it's of no use anymore.' The priest (Darroussin, not dressed as a priest) then turns to the camera, breaking the impression of a coherent fiction, and tells the viewer directly that the story will go from bad to good: 'At the beginning of this story, the world was horrible; it's hard to imagine it now.' He also gives a precise numerical breakdown of the situation. 'Three months ago', there were 'in this housing project, 953 inhabitants: 456 unemployed, 302 alcoholics, 251 thieves, 220 fascists, 220 Muslim fundamentalists [*intégristes*], 192 drug addicts, fifty-nine people with AIDS, just three communists, and myself, the priest.' This is one of Guédiguian's most Brechtian films, and here the prologue presents the situation from after the conflict, so that it can be historicised.

An extreme high-angle shot, panning from the industrial port to the public housing project where the film is set (such shots are found in most of Guédiguian's films) establishes its singularity and emphasises its isolation, like a stage set representing a number of problems of French society in 1992. The priest comments as the camera leads into nearly identical apartments to introduce the characters of this ensemble film: we meet Simona Viali (Ascaride), the spunky widow of a burglar, who sells stolen goods from her home; Muñoz (Meylan), the former accomplice to Simona's husband who now works as a bank guard with his German shepherd (Muñoz is now one of the fascists); the North African Amzoula family, with an unemployed and 'fundamentalist' father (Hamzaoui) and their happy-go-lucky son Mourad; the Degros family, headed by one of the three communists, ashamed of his own son, the imprisoned 'Caïd' of the complex. These families are linked together: sometimes by a shared history, long-ago friendship (Degros and the others) or sentimental attachment (Degros's daughter is in love with Simona's son, Pierre, but loved by Mourad).

The narrative, told through flashback, finds this community in full crisis: Degros's son Jacques has been put into prison for dealing drugs, and, while he is gone, his two 'lieutenants', Simona's son Pierre and Omar of the Amzoula family battle for territorial control. They divide the projects literally, with a yellow line painted down the middle of the courtyard, and forbid their gangs from crossing it. Tension spins out of control in ways that are both funny and disturbing: Pierre dumps Isabelle and steals everything from his mother; when he sees Isabelle and Mourad spending time together he accidentally shoots Mourad; most of the kids declare war, but when other kids throw household objects out of windows one child is severely injured and blood flows from his head. This spiral downward nearly spins out of control and poses a threat to Guédiguian's narrative constraint: 'humour, no deaths, and a positive ending'.

The film draws the viewer's full attention to the arbitrary and artificial line: a non-diegetic Rossini violin concerto plays in counterpoint as the kids paint it, and it is often shown from an abstract, high-angle perspective, including at night, when it has a translucent glow. Again, this is a Brechtian effect: the line is allegorical and suggests that the problems are entirely self-inflicted. But it also sparks a reaction among some of the more thoughtful residents. First, the priest tries first to induce a moral conscience in the inhabitants. To the young Isabelle, he explains what it means to be a priest: 'Croire, ça fait aimer les autres' ('Believing makes you love others'), and conjugal deprivation turns the 'heat of the blood' into a spiritual passion. He has set up shop in a corrugated shed in the courtyard, where he crosses the spatial division, preaches to the inhabitants and distributes clean needles; but, though he can speak ideologically, in his own name, the priest is rather ineffective, a kind of Jeremiah, standing in the courtyard to berate people tired of listening to him. The reaction of the women, led by Simona, is more impactful. Like the priest, she turns the courtyard into a theatre for political speech, pleading with the inhabitants to pull together in solidarity. Later, she invites the other women from the block to meet in the tin chapel, where they plot ways of crossing the line. Madame Degros (Frédérique Bonnal) threatens to leave her husband if he doesn't make peace with his imprisoned son. Muñoz's wife begs him to quit his job as a security guard and become a thief again (she found him more attractive when he wasn't a fascist). Madame Amzoula takes over the family space and interrupts her husband's morning prayer to convince him to stop spending time with the radical Islamists. Even the elderly Madame Morel sneaks out at night to retouch the swastikas painted on the estate walls so that they look like whimsical faces with snot running out their noses. The painted-on line of separation is therefore undergoing a transformation: it is provoking an emergent community attempting to resist its divisiveness.

This resistance, indicative of the new direction in Guédiguian's cinema, again resonates profoundly with the work of Ernst Bloch. In *The Principle of Hope*, Bloch integrates the happy ending into larger theories of hope and utopia. Bloch argues that human beings, engaged in the struggle for life, have a forward-oriented relation to time with a desire to change unfavourable conditions. This desire shapes a consciousness 'which overhauls the available world in the imagination' (Bloch 1995: 76). The imagination is a glimpse into the 'not-yet-conscious', related to a flourishing future: '*The not-yet-conscious as a whole is the psychological representation of the Not-Yet-Become in an age and its world, on the Front of the world*' (italics in the original, Bloch 1995: 127). In the 'psychological birthplace of the New', we form images of difference and a better life. The imagination perceives limits – like the line across the courtyard – as something to overcome: 'Every barrier, when it is felt as such, is at the same time crossed' (Bloch 1995: 444). By transforming the housing block into an abstract and divided space, Guédiguian provides an elegant illustration of the workings of Blochian imagination.

The imagination comes armed with many strategies for crossing barriers, of which one is daydream, which Bloch distinguishes forcefully from the night dreams so important to Freud: 'the daydreamer often follows will-o'-the-wisps, gets led astray. But he is not asleep and does not sink back down with the mist' (Bloch 1995: 78). Near the end of the film, Viali, as a ghost, comes to visit Simona and gives her the idea for a spectacular bank robbery that will unite the community in a shared project. Beyond a playful camera sweep from the blue sky to her apartment, there are no diegetic markers that Simona is 'dreaming': it is her desire for a change in the housing block that provokes her imagination of a more flourishing life, and she pursues it. The last twenty minutes of the film are devoted to the preparation and successful execution of the farcical robbery, including everyone from the kids (posing as orphans) to the priest, the communist, the fascist Muñoz and his German shepherd, and Ascaride dressed as a nun.

This renewed community spirit enables them to leave behind the artificial line dividing the housing project and focus on a more real economic division, the one separating the projects from the banks and other institutions that profit from the social organisation. Throughout most of the film, this outside barely registers: it is like a hidden god going merrily along its way while the housing block suffers inner turmoil. But after the bank robbery they leave the stolen bus they had used in a dusty lot: a new line of separation, the frontier between them and those who profit while they suffer and which will now receive their full attention. Organised against it, the community can now come together in a scene of comic resolution: Isabelle marries Pierre under Mourad's approving gaze; and even the priest and Simona have a kiss. Like a Frank Capra film, the good win in the end and even get (relatively) rich.

The film reflects Bloch's efforts to recuperate the happy ending in his writings on popular culture. On one hand, Bloch denounces the traditional happy ending as an illusion of a capitalistic society, where, typically, the good end up rich while the evil or weak end up in the slums, prisons or hungry. This false hope, or 'merry swindle', is always expressed in the achievement of immediate gratification or status and has little to do with Aristotelian 'eudaimonia': 'shallower than at any other time, [the happy end] confines itself to the smile of the car and perfume advertisements' (Bloch 1995: 442). But Bloch does not completely dismiss the happy ending: 'an unmistakable drive is working in the direction of the good end, it is not only confined to gullibility' (1995: 442). In fact, he prefers even the false happy ending to 'unconditional pessimism', which tends to 'immortalize the trudging of the little life' or 'give humanity the face of a chloroformed gravestone' (Bloch 1995: 445). Bloch uses vague language to describe a more historically authentic happy ending, but this is because hope is related to virtualities to be created rather than obvious *idées reçues*: '[Truth's] attitude is, becomes, remains criticalmilitant optimism, and this orientates itself in the Become always towards the Not-Yet-Become, towards viable possibilities of the light' (Bloch 1995: 446).

For Guédiguian, *L'Argent fait le bonheur* is an unrealistic film because it does not show suffering as destiny: 'it had to be totally unrealistic, or else the housing project would be filled with flame and blood and covered with dead bodies' (Danel 2008: 73). Instead, it attempts to envision an action that might lead to a future becoming. Though robbing a bank may at first seem like immediate gratification, the point of this happy ending is obviously not the money but, informed by 'critical-militant optimism', the renewed community of friends and their creative resistance; or as Viali puts it: 'family, the block, and friends'. For the first time, Guédiguian calls this film a 'conte', or 'tale' – later he will specify 'contes de L'Estaque' ('Tales from L'Estaque') – again echoing Bloch, for whom the fairy tale, like the daydream and happy ending, is one of the innumerable manifestations of utopian thinking.

À la vie, à la mort! (1995)

Like *L'Argent fait le bonheur*, *À la vie, à la mort!* aims 'to show that one can still fight in some way or another, even if it is at a microscopic level' (Danel 2008: 80). This film, however, is not billed as a *conte*: its characters struggle with a sobering economic situation, one that Guédiguian explores from the opening shot. The film opens at night, the camera in a car moving through Leclerc shopping centres, Géant supermarkets, gas stations and factory outlets. The shaky images combined with a soundtrack of the 'Blue Danube' make a derisive comment on kitschy consumerism. These are spaces of precarity and underemployment, where people working for minimum wage must drive themselves to work, roads leading nowhere from nowhere. We are caught in a flow of movement, without past or future, lost in the gaudy lights of the present, reflecting well what Laura Rascaroli calls 'the end of geography', i.e. the 'irrelevance of place in the contemporary socio-economic and technological contexts' and the 'disappearance of the cities of the past' (Rascaroli 2006: 96).

The credits emphasise Guédiguian's ensemble approach: first, we see Agat Films & Cie, and then the cast, in alphabetical order, the entire band of collaborators, gathered in equality. This contrasts sharply with the next shot, which contains just one individual. A politician or a union leader (Pierre Banderet), dressed like a used-car salesman, speaks from multiple televisions stacked in a window (probably at one of the box stores we have already seen), the mouthpiece of capital multiplied, replacing our group of friends. He claims to have roots in the working class but insists that the long-term restructuring of the economy requires us to stop fighting 'les entrepreneurs' according to old 'schemas'. He then states a phrase that will be repeated throughout the film: 'C'est tous ensemble qu'on fabriquera le bel avenir à nos enfants. Croyez moi.'[3] He embodies the entrepreneurial attitude that life is investment: sacrifice now will pay off in the future.

This film again insists on the importance of place, a stable, unmoving place, in contrast with the opening flow of traffic: the Perroquet Bleu, a bar situated between factories and the sea, between industry and the Mediterranean.[4] We are again outside society, in an anchor against the flows of capital. Inside the bar we find gathered at any given moment the ensemble of characters: Josiane, an ageing stripper (played by sixty-two-year-old Pascale Roberts); Patrick (Jacques Gamblin), unemployed, who cannot give his wife Marie-Sol (Ascaride) a child because he is sterile; José (Meylan), owner of the

3 'It is all together that we build a beautiful future for our children, believe me.'
4 The name comes from a bar that Guédiguian would pass by as a child in Marseilles. The space itself will be familiar to viewers of Guédiguian's cinema, since various scenes have been shot here, as well as most of *Au fil d'Ariane* (2013). It is again introduced with a sweeping pan from the bay over L'Estaque.

Perroquet Bleu, Marie-Sol's brother and Josiane's husband, who pays a young drug addict, Vénus (Laetitia Pesenti) for sex, and whose business is failing, in part because Josiane is ageing; Jaco (Darroussin), also unemployed, whose marital troubles began when he lost his job, now sinking into alcoholism and homelessness; and Otto (Jacques Pieiller), a German-origin former legionnaire, who is also a closeted gay man. Rounding out the characters is Papa Carlosa, Josiane and Jaco's father (Boudet), who cannot walk because of an accident and is approaching senescence (he seems lost in memories of fighting against Franco in Spain), and Vénus's young friend, Farid (Farid Ziane).

Their economic troubles, especially long-term unemployment, are presented with precision. But the film concentrates mostly on the emotional effects of precarity: anger, anxiety (Patrick worrying about the future) and alienation (Jaco becomes homeless and loses contact with his friends).[5] Among those emotional problems, the film provides a particularly astute analysis of how precarity affects sexual relationships. On one hand, the spectacle of the striptease is presented as a space in which fantasy allows men to forget their economic woes. José and Jaco, for example, jokingly sing a song and dance like strippers: with each discarded piece of clothing disappears some economic worry; off comes a glove and goodbye taxes, then goodbye unemployment, goodbye boss and so on. But sex also mixes with economic power: Marie-Sol must quit her job as a housekeeper when her boss tries to force her to have sex with him, making everyone's economic situation even worse. Jaco drinks, and when he tries to interest his wife she tells him to 'get to work first'; he answers in anger and frustration by punching her, and she leaves him.

Their present difficulties push concerns for the past and future out of view. Papa Carlosa represents a militant past in which he fought in the resistance against Franco in Spain. But he had a serious work accident in France and spends his days in a wheelchair, his enfeebled

5 Guy Standing's work on precaritised mind identifies several emotional issues that are common to the large swathes of society that he calls the 'precariat', many of which are linked to the constant preoccupation with how the bills will be paid at the present moment and where one will find the next bit of income. Generally people living with precarity lose self-esteem, in great part because they lose 'trusting relationships' (Standing 2011: 22), the *philia* that make them feel as if they are living a worthwhile life.

mind having trouble distinguishing between now and then. With great pains he works at a reproducing a painting that he can never get right in marker on the family refrigerator. It resembles Goya's famous *Third of May 1804*, commemorating the Spanish resistance to Joseph Napoléon's rule of Spain and Murat's occupation. Goya's painting depicts the execution of a resistance fighter by Murat's soldiers, the fighter on the left of the painting and the soldiers on the right. Painted in 1814, after the expulsion of the French, the painting expresses a defiant heroism. But throughout most of the film Papa Carlosa can only come up with half of the painting, showing the dying resister clumsily drawn in marker on the refrigerator door.

If Papa Carlosa represents a weak link to a militant past, an uncertain future is obviously symbolised in the child that Patrick cannot father. Guédiguian takes pains to de-emphasise the biological problem (and the personal melodrama that it could provoke) and treats the childbearing as a collective endeavour. Everybody wants a child: José cannot have one with Josiane, who is too old; Jaco's daughters hate him for hitting their mom and disappear with her; Otto is a closeted gay man; and Patrick's sterility is vaguely associated with his depression. Papa Carlosa declares that without children there is 'nothing', no reason to continue. Looking for a miracle, Marie-Sol prays to the statue of Mary at the Notre-Dame de la Garde basilica for help, but friendship resolves the biological problem: she asks Jaco, her adoptive brother, to sleep with her, and she conceives.

In the end, they all will pull together to support the child. Even José announces that he has sold his beloved Mercedes for cash. The film thus redefines the family away from consanguinity towards a larger group of friends who work together to assure each other's future, of which the child is the manifestation. An image of *philia* shines through their interactions: Josépha is a stripper, but the other characters respect her and her work (even if Marie-Sol does not want to be one herself); José most of all loves her deeply, even though he pays Vénus for sex. He takes advantage of Vénus, but their sexual relationship ends quickly, and, along with Farid, to whom he has become a father figure, he helps her kick her addiction. The depressed Patrick does not turn violent like Jaco or indulge in sexual escapism, even when he suspects Marie-Sol is pregnant by someone else; instead, he continues to collect sea urchins for her and to take care of her father. She thanks him for not turning mean when he lost his job ('When you're kind it gives me courage'). Even Papa Carlosa manages to finish his painting. Deep ties keep them striving to love each other as best they can, and they all come to live in the home of this new family, in what has become another, utopian space: the Perroquet Bleu.

In the film's most comic and endearing scenes, this community helps Patrick work through jealousy and accept the redefined family in the last part of the film. Though Guédiguian is frequently critical of Marcel Pagnol's *Marius* trilogy, Patrick bears a resemblance to Panisse, a comic character who agrees to marry Fanny, abandoned but pregnant with Marius's child, and accepts to raise her child as his own. One of the most Pagnolesque moments in Guédiguian's film comes when Jaco, José and their friend Otto tease Patrick about the changes in Marie-Sol's body. The camera cuts from face to face to underline the nearly transparent double entendre to highly comic effect. ('Patrick, don't you think Marie-Sol has taken on a little belly, like a football?') They even use the Pagnolesque term 'cocu' ('cuckold'). Here Patrick is alone for a moment, standing in the crossfire of his friends' gentle mockery. He is, however, treated sympathetically by the other characters: Papa Carlosa jokes with him; Marie-Sol is particularly kind; and Farid tells him he's not stupid or mean but 'un mec bien' ('a good bloke').

At such moments, the film comes close to the *conte de L'Estaque* aesthetic. But globally it is too dark, with many scenes shot at twilight, in the bar, under the bridge where Jaco sleeps or in the streets at night. The Mediterranean sun appears briefly, especially on the terrace, but even then the film is wintery, the characters bundled up and cold. The film is a constant struggle between dark and light, and its light is much more fragile. The entire group gathers around the pregnant Marie-Sol when José pulls out his large roll of cash, but in a dramatic effect the lights immediately go out in the Perroquet Bleu: they are months behind in paying electricity, in danger of losing their anchor against the displacing flow of the economy.

The film ends at least three times, each reacting to Patrick's suicide and each stressing solidarity. The act itself takes place in a beautiful scene filmed at dusk.[6] It is a recurring figure in Guédiguian's work

---

6 It contrasts with another scene in which Vénus, 'reborn' and purified in her recovery, wades nude in the water with Vivaldi on the soundtrack, an obvious citation of Botticelli's *Birth of Venus*.

to show friends swimming in the sea, but Patrick has always been afraid of the water, and here he stands alone. He removes his clothes, carefully folds them and places his watch on the pile: a gesture reminiscent of Marcel Carné's *Quai des brumes* (1938), in which a painter drowns himself, leaving behind identity papers and a neatly folded bundle of clothes so that Jean Gabin might have a new identity. Patrick is entirely nude, with the remnants of the sunset casting his body in a soft light, highlighted with the darker purple of the impending night: there is hope as well as death in the image. A voiceover of Patrick reading a letter to Marie-Sol links this image to the following group shot of the other characters walking slowly, with each face visible, from his grave. He clarifies that he is not killing himself out of jealousy ('you may think I'm doing this because I am cuckolded, but you're wrong'), but so that she and the others can cash in his life-insurance policy. Patrick has sacrificed himself for the future, just as the man on the television had wanted. But even this Christ-like sacrifice is fragile and temporary: he calculates that the insurance will pay out enough for the others to keep the bar for exactly two years and eight months.

Another cut brings the friends back to the Perroquet Bleu, once again facing the sea in a wintry Mediterranean light, in an ending that now recuperates the past and points to resistance. This scene illustrates one of Guédiguian's preferred motifs, the meal scene, and here the very decision to share a meal indicates a willingness to continue, the seed of a resistance developed in the rest of the scene. Through tears and clinking plates, as the camera frames the group around the table, Papa Carlosa begins to sing. The camera zooms through the group to the back of the old man's head, filling the frame with it as the others' voices rise. The song, 'Ay Carmela', is a rallying hymn dating from the anti-fascist resistance in Spain. Papa Carlosa seems to be awoken from senescence by the continuity of Patrick's act with his own past. And his reaction is contagious, as the other voices join in with the rousing refrain ('la rumba, la rumba, la rumba'). If there is any movement forward it will have to come from banding together in solidarity, in mutual help, in memory of past resistance, themes that will be developed in Guédiguian's subsequent work, especially *Marius et Jeannette*.

The final ending points towards the future: an obviously pregnant Marie-Sol removes the ex-voto she had left in the chapel of the basilica. The shot carries over Guédiguian's self-conscious use of religion from *L'Argent fait le bonheur*, in which the priest seems to leave the church for love of Simona: in both films, religious fervour contributes positively to the group unity but in the end is abandoned for the group itself (as it will be later in *Mon père est ingénieur*). Marie-Sol (Marie of the Earth) lives up to her name: the camera pans down her front to show her stomach in the foreground, the city lights in the background, the focus shifting from her belly to the city. The comment of the politician from the beginning of the film, heard one last time on the soundtrack, now becomes strangely appropriate, or perhaps appropriated, to the film's call for solidarity: 'it's all together that we will construct a beautiful future for our children, believe me.' The film finally ends on this amplification from Marie-Sol's situation to the collective city – the city absent from the opening shots – its chiaroscuro indicating the need for people willing to stand firmly against the flows of capital, in resistance, such as one finds in the seedy but luminous Perroquet Bleu.

A film finds its moment

L'Argent fait le bonheur was a television film that had a modicum of success on the festival circuit, whereas *À la vie, à la mort!*, Guédiguian's most popular film at the time, was viewed by approximately 120,000 people. Guédiguian's work was beginning to discover an audience, but it was an immense leap to the sensational success of *Marius et Jeannette*. This film was fêted early at Cannes, where it opened the *Un certain regard* parallel selection, won the prix Louis Delluc and the prix Lumières, and was nominated for several César awards (including a win for best actress for Ariane Ascaride). At over 2.5 million spectators, it was one of the highest grossing French films of 1997 and still accounts for about a third of Guédiguian's viewership over his entire career. Earlier films were rebroadcast on television, and Guédiguian and his actors were suddenly appearing on award shows and being interviewed in media outlets.

To some degree, the film's success can be attributed to a shifting political environment, two years into Jacques Chirac's first term, in which Guédiguian's message of *philia* and micro-revolution touched a nerve. Chirac won that election in part by exploiting an ambiguous discourse on 'la fracture sociale' ('social fracture'), which led, after his election, to reinforcement of the anti-immigration Pasqua laws with the Debré law (one of its main provisions required citizens to report undocumented immigrants to the town hall). Phil Powrie gives a detailed account of how the film industry had made a cause of defending the *sans-papiers* during this period (see Powrie 1999: 11 and following): on 11 February, sixty-six directors protested during a news conference, and *Le Monde* and *Libération* published a text written by Pascale Ferran and Arnaud Desplechin and signed by many others. The signatories openly avowed that they would continue to 'shelter, not to denounce, to sympathise with, and to work with our friends and colleagues without checking that their papers are in order'.[7]

Guédiguian had produced some of Ferran's work, and, according to his account, Ferran and Desplechin's idea to write the letter took form in discussions in the offices of Agat Films & Cie (Sahuc 2011: 53). Guédiguian partially credits the efforts there for Chirac's defeat, in 1997, when he dissolved the National Assembly only to lose his majority and be forced into a cohabitation government with the socialist prime minister Lionel Jospin: 'je crois modestement que ça a contribué au succès de la gauche aux élections' (Sahuc 2011: 53).[8] Guédiguian's version of the story reflects his ideal of a reinvigorated but unaffiliated political activism, a reinvention of politics rather than a return to old narratives. In a number of texts published in the month following the petition, the directors show an acute awareness of 'the collapse of traditional left-wing party politics' and, in Guédiguian's words, a 'militantisme de proximité' (translated by Powrie as 'community politics'; Powrie 1999: 12). The growing link between politics and cinema culminated at the 1997 Cannes Festival where several film-makers agreed to show, before their films were screened, a short film of a young African woman named Traoré describing her immigration case (see Powrie 1999: 14 and Sahuc 2011: 54). Opening up *Un certain regard* with *Marius et Jeannette* meant that Guédiguian was the first to present this film. It is not a coincidence that *Marius et Jeannette* would benefit from this political environment: many of Guédiguian's ideas on local politics and small-scale film-making

---

7 Translation by Powrie. (See Powrie 1999: 10–11 for details on the protest.)
8 'I humbly believe that it contributed in a small way to the success of the left in the elections.'

were in fact honed in 1995 and 1996, during a long tour of screening and debates of *À la vie, à la mort!*, and would be applied in *Marius et Jeannette*, which was completed in 1996.[9]

Marius et Jeannette (1997)

One of Guédiguian's conclusions at the end of the debates around *À la vie, à la mort!* was that he wanted to make 'the smallest film possible' (Danel 2008: 83). *Marius et Jeannette* recounts a budding love between two eponymous characters, played by Ascaride and Meylan, roughed up by personal loss and economic hardship. Jeannette's home opens onto a small courtyard, shared by her, her two kids (by different fathers) and a number of neighbours: Caroline (a communist survivor of German concentration camps), Justin (a retired schoolteacher), Monique and Dédé (a couple with three children who bicker constantly over a vote he once made for the Front National). Jeannette and Marius fall in love, and the others in the community accept Marius among them. One day he disappears, but, with help from the friends, he reconciles with Jeannette: the bond of the couple comes from the bond of the community; the everyday is enchanted. This is the smallest film possible, but, as Steven Ungar has noted, one that aspires to universality through its use of the romantic comedy.

Guédiguian's artistry is generally underappreciated, but here, in particular, he combines a nimble touch with a surprisingly complex *mise en scène* that rewards close reading. The slightly absurd pre-title sequence begins with a blank screen and, on the soundtrack, a traditional-sounding '*farandole*' ('Il pleut sur Marseille') as Ungar identifies it, a Provençale dance in 6/8 time (Ungar 2000: 41). The first

9 The film was also blessed by practical circumstances. Pierre Chevalier, from Arte, proposed a short television film. With Milesi he quickly wrote a screenplay and shot the film, in about five weeks, working 'no more than five hours a day' (Danel 2008: 84). They filmed in L'Estaque, in the courtyard where Malek Hamzaoui had grown up and where Guédiguian and Meylan had spent many hours as teenagers. Everyone was available, the entire troupe as it was constituted at the time appears, and virtually every face in the film is either recognisable from previous films or a personal friend or relative: the credit sequence lists only recognisable names. Even one of the main visual motifs of the film – the destruction of the cement works – was a total coincidence integrated into the screenplay.

images show a beach ball floating into harbour, past a Mediterranean ferry and over an inexplicably submerged direction arrow indicating L'Estaque, until it eventually hits land. The ball is transparent but has images of the continents printed on it, in the style of a globe, floating upside down. Both Ungar and Powrie read the sequence as a movement from the global towards the local, and both point out the importance of Pagnol and his *Marius* trilogy as signifiers of Marseilles regionalism. However, Guédiguian's stance here is not one of regional nostalgia but rather an argument for the politics of proximity. The small transparent globe would represent the ideology of globalisation being pursued aggressively in 1997, returning to l'Estaque, a forgotten local space (even its signpost is sunk in the port). The film deconstructs Pagnol's *Marius* (1931) at least in one sense, since Pagnol's Marius (Pierre Fresnay) cannot bear to stay in Marseilles and leaves on a merchant marine ship to see the world. Here that desire comes back as detritus, upside down, filled with air, landing in the place that has suffered from it. Even the song, though it sounds traditional, is a new, rough-around-the-edges version, co-written by Milesi. Thus the nostalgic and regional are globalised and politically lucid: the local is opposed to the global but not closed to difference.[10] The prologue thus introduces the issue of scale, the relation between the local and the global, whose effects on the local are felt just after the credits.

A blunt cut shows a wrecking crane destroying a wall of the cement works; without a visible operator, it resembles a metal dinosaur demolishing the wall, driven by its own appetite. Guédiguian plays with register here: the crushing sound contrasts with the farandole: we have left the absurd atmosphere and entered a realistic film about the ravages of the global economy (the factory jobs have left for elsewhere). Jeannette's first meeting with Marius illustrates how human interaction plays out in this world. She cannot afford to buy paint to touch up her home on her cashier's salary, so she breaks into the factory yard to steal a couple of cans rusting in a corner.[11]

---

10 Powrie (2001), playing with the notion of transparency, also sees a number of tensions in the film played out through the ball (between universalism and regionalism; between utopia and realism; between the outwardness of utopia and the inwardness of nostalgia).

11 Painting the house is obviously symbolic as well, as is clear again later when Jeannette and Marius do a completely unrealistic job painting it (right over the old peeling paint and spilling new paint all over the floor).

Tall, unkempt, limping and armed with a rifle, Marius is frightening, like the wrecking crane. He defines for Jeannette the social roles that hold in this economic system: first, the paint does not belong to him or her but to the company (even if it will never be used); he also demands Jeannette's papers, showing that power can be exploited along lines of race or immigration, even if she is obviously not an immigrant.[12] Jeannette can only defend herself with language, a sassy argument that nobody cares about the paint and that he's acting like a fascist. Economic power continues to weigh on Jeannette into the next scene, where she is slumped in her seat at work at the supermarket, watching two buckets of paint move slowly towards her on the conveyor, linking the two spaces in a single system of ownership and control from which she is excluded.

The next sequence moves consciously away from this economic world with another panning shot floating over rooftops and the return of farandole, strongly establishing this different, local space, the courtyard, with its soft evening light and pink roses in bloom. This space is the central kernel of the film, and Guédiguian approaches it in many ways. First, it is a place in which people and things are transformed from commodities in the economy into what they are for human affect. When Jeannette hears a sound at the courtyard gate, the camera playfully cuts from inside: we see the paint sitting on the ground with Jeannette's crossed legs as she leans against the wall, then a cut to a cleaned-up Marius who says hello, a countershot to Jeannette, back and forth as Marius explains that that the paint is for her, following the eye line Jeannette seductively thanks him; as Marius limps away she smiles in close-up. Here Marius shows himself, and even the paint is knitted, by the editing itself, into the fabric of a human relationship. Ten minutes later we will see Marius and Jeannette repainting her ceiling together.

The film continuously undoes stereotypes and viewer expectations, cinematic images and cultural figures. Take minority stereotyping: when we see Jeannette's family for the first time and hear her lecturing her African-fathered son about grades, this fits into a system of stereotypes – of course he would be a weak student, and yet

12 In the following film, À la place du cœur, Guédiguian will show that a young black man, asked the same question, this time by a cop, does not have the leeway to answer back.

we find out that he is third in his class and later will become a professor. (He is also physically weak, undermining another stereotype.)[13] It also turns out that Magali's white father left Jeannette, whereas Malek's father was killed in an accident, undercutting the stereotype that men of colour are unreliable. Marius appears not only as the guardian of company property but also as a handicapped person, probably because of an industrial accident. But when he challenges Jeannette to a foot race he stops limping and easily wins, an echo of another foot race involving the disguised Jeanne Moreau in Truffaut's *Jules et Jim* (1962). Marius explains that the handicap was an invention to get his job by making the interviewer feel sorry for him. His scowl, his anger and his limp are mere masks.[14]

The courtyard is of the scale that Rascaroli calls the 'lodging', 'the most significant and original spatial category' in Guédiguian's work, but it is also slightly larger than a traditional home since it is both closed and protected and open to a larger society (Rascaroli 2006: 99). It is one of the 'communist' spaces; indeed, the most accomplished of these utopian spaces that also include the café in *Dernier été*, the Perroquet Bleu, or the gardens in *Ki lo sa?* Guédiguian's treatment of the courtyard is reminiscent of Renoir's *Le Crime de Monsieur Lange* (1936) in that it takes on central importance, though here the characters are not subordinate to space but the source of its meaning.[15] Guédiguian's camera does not bother mapping out the space of the courtyard but instead follows the lines of human relations that structure it affectively, in some ways contrary to *L'Argent fait le bonheur*, where the space was entirely abstract. We see Justin (Boudet) sitting

13 The film does suggest that his view of the world comes from support at home: in a different scene, Marius, while helping a group of kids repair a bicycle, asks them what they want to be later, to which each of them answers, in comical succession, 'a football player'.
14 M. Ébrard, Jeannette's boss, offers an interesting counterpoint. Early in the film he lords over Jeannette and the other cashiers, eventually firing her. But midway through the film he returns, this time in the courtyard, selling women's underwear door-to-door to support his rather fat wife and numerous children. The women of the courtyard feel sorry for him and make a purchase, though Jeannette writes him a bad cheque. Later he appears at a restaurant as a waiter, where it comes out that he has never had a family. Ébrard is thus all appearance, conforming to whatever figure might preserve his position in the economy (though he still ends up a victim).
15 See André Bazin's reading of the relationship between the courtyard and the characters in Renoir's film (Bazin 1986: 45).

on his steps reading. (We hear chirruping cicadas, almost ubiquitous in Guédiguian's films.)[16] A cut to Caroline (Pascale Roberts), about his age, with a communist-Resistance background, who calls Jeannette's name and steps out onto her own steps. We see Caroline and Jeannette from Justin's eye line as they talk about Castro's visit to France; another cut shows Justin observing from his balcony. Then a cut to Jeannette in the alley, off to find a new job: she bumps into Dédé (Darroussin) coming back from work, and the camera follows him back into the courtyard as a bouncy tune replaces the sound of the insects. Dédé ignores his children in the courtyard and plants himself in a folding chair, until another character shows up.

The space is also non-homogenous: people of different genders, generations, levels of intelligence and, to a lesser degree, ethnic origins inhabit it and encounter each other, in a space of trust and comfort conducive to conversation and critique. At times, the camera films straight on, as in the theatre, illustrating Guédiguian's manner of staging political dialogue: Dédé sits down, his wife Monique (Frédérique Bonnal) pops her head out of a window behind him, and they argue about a strike he is supposed to begin with his colleagues; light falls in a diagonal across the front of their house dividing them; she disappears and reappears at another window, reproaching him for once having voted Front National; he asks what good it does to stop working, and she replies, hyperbolically, that the last strike 'saved social security'; Dédé storms off as Justin arrives and begins dancing with the kids in celebration of a teachers' strike. The space also becomes pedagogical, as when Justin explains religious differences to Malek, who now identifies as a Muslim in honour of his dead father.[17] It is also a space of transmission: often the women

16 Justin likes to read *Le Monde Diplomatique*, one of the leading anti-globalisation papers, whereas Caroline prefers *L'Humanité*, the Communist paper.
17 Justin gives a traditionally republican argument concerning the relation of religion to politics. Malek asks Justin why there are so many religions. Justin offers Marseilles as a comparison, but a Marseilles that would represent all of humanity: there are people from this neighbourhood or that, but they are still all Marseillais. Later, a cut will show Justin in close-up, a bright sky behind him, the image of authority, as he explains to Malek and a friend the difference between religion and fundamentalism: to paraphrase, the fundamentalist, of all religions, seeks power by exploiting and refusing difference (he calls the fundamentalist the 'colour-blind' of religion). It is perhaps an obvious lesson but one not without political significance given the events of 1997.

gather under Justin's gaze on the steps leading to Caroline's apartment, where she tells stories of her time in a Nazi camp. Romantic love is a private joy but also a topic for public concern: the friends in the courtyard want Jeannette to find love because it is a joy they feel she deserves.[18] The courtyard is a vector of encounters: it can offer fun and solace and allows the friends to develop meaning in their lives.

Guédiguian also combines daily life with fantasy to give the courtyard a dream-like quality. When Marius arrives with the paint, a cut brings the viewer to a daydream sequence, where in typical Harlequin romance style (over-brilliant colours accompanied by an operatic 'O solé mio' on the soundtrack), Jeannette imagines herself on a beach. Marius, in his watchman's red work overalls, runs towards her, without a limp, and they embrace.[19] Guédiguian also uses the uncanny. Jeanette spends her first night with Marius but finds it strange that they do not have sex. Back in the courtyard, Monique, in an incongruous remark that earns her confused looks, comments that Marius must not go to the cinema very often, since there people just have sex all the time, even standing up in the mud. But several scenes later, we hear 'O'solé mio' again, and we see Jeannette dressing and a naked Marius. They are outside, or rather within the walls of an overgrown ruin. Marius is standing in the mud: it is not a daydream this time (though the setting and soundtrack may suggest just that), but actually occurs in the narrative world. Reality, dream and cinema intertwine, with the additional self-conscious touch that the scene is played out in a film. The scene is evoked again in a speech made by Caroline, recalling sex in the German camps. Once again she describes being 'barefoot, in the mud, leaning against the barbed wire'. She adds that sex was 'dream-like' and that it was perhaps the only thing that kept her and her fellow prisoners, the communists,

---

18 Love and sex are important themes for every generation: Justin and Caroline demonstrate that desire does not end when one ages; Jeannette falls in love despite not wanting more children; she shares a frank discussion of sex with Magali, to whom she gives the lingerie she has bought from M. Ébrard; and even Malek gets a talk from Justin about how God does not care if he masturbates.

19 We cut back to her in close-up in the courtyard, smiling about her daydream, which is then negated by the next scene of Jeannette at work and Ébrard asking her if she is 'daydreaming' again.

from losing hope: making love was their last vestige of freedom. Watching the film, we feel that we are in a realist universe but one steeped in fantasy, resistance and history.

The important question in the plot is whether or not Marius can be integrated into this community. Again the use of sound, camera and editing shows that this is a possibility, at least in the courtyard setting. Justin steps out of his door and calls 'hello' to Caroline across the way (the cicadas are still chirping); the camera pans to her response as we hear 'O'solé mio' whistled in the distance. We then cut into Jeannette's house: she is scraping paint off the floor, barefoot and wearing a 'bleu de travail' and starts to sing 'O'solé mio' (fantasy becomes real life) as the camera pans to link her to an identically clad Marius, source of the whistling. A new cut, with Jeannette's voice still singing, brings us back to Caroline and Justin, in shot countershot, watching each other and then having a flirty conversation about the beans. Eventually Caroline will invite Justin to share them for dinner. Another cut, and, in the evening, we hear Dédé and Monique cursing at each other about the Front National again while the camera pans again, up to Caroline's balcony, where a dapper Justin and alluring Caroline are finishing their meal. They speak frankly about making love to each other many years earlier. (Again the sound of crickets.) They come together in the same shot for the first time, like Marius and Jeannette just before. Actions are not separate; stories are not discrete; sounds and images overlap. As Caroline says, quoting Justin back to him, 'Everything is linked to everything.'

One of the specialties of Guédiguian's *mise en scène*, the meal scene, is particularly well represented in this film and is elastic enough to allow him to explore levels of cohesion between characters and their relation to various spaces. One scene shows the characters' discomfort away from the courtyard. It begins with the view of a lake, with the Strauss waltz in the background. The camera begins to zoom out. The effect is not to efface the lake but to bring us away from it and include the image of two diners, soon included in the frame: they are a professional couple, talking about French regulations, European exchanges and other minutiae of international finance. The frame continues to widen to include Marius and Jeannette, also at the margins of the image, now in foreground, listening to but not comprehending the other couple. Jeannette cannot find prices on the menu, so Marius explains that he has the one with the prices; he also has to explain the difference between the water and wine glass and the use of other utensils. The oddness of this entry into the space of the restaurant terrace repeats Jeannette's discomfort in her foray into the leisure spaces of high finance: eating has its own class rules that she cannot comprehend. (Marius only knows the etiquette because he was a waiter for a couple of summers.) This meal takes place in the world in which they are out of place, but it also brings them closer together.[20]

The second sequence, during which the friends make an aioli, explores Marius's possible entry into the group. The scene takes place at the factory, which is transformed into a communal space by their meal. In contrast to the fine fare of the restaurant, aioli is a meal that brings people together to work: the men buy ingredients for Monique's recipe and make the aioli sauce while the women prepare the eggs, fish and vegetables that will be dipped. (Note the subtle reversal of gender roles, despite the separation into two groups: the men follow Monique's recipe and do the shopping.) Aioli itself is a combination of flavours, a mixture of differences reflected in the shots of Dédé and Marius mixing it. The scene invites the viewer to consider the differences harmoniously gathered here as well: different generations, ranging from the kids to Justin and Caroline, and different tastes (the men have trouble accepting fennel in the aioli). At the end of the meal, we hear 'Il pleut sur Marseille' once again, but then Malek replaces the cassette (diegetic and non-diegetic worlds mix again) with the same song played in a modern rock style; the above-angle shot transforms the lot into a kind of abstract or theatrical mixing bowl (there are several circular motifs in the shot) in which everyone dances, the bright and varying colours of their clothes creating once again the impression of diversity coming together.[21]

Marius, however, remains the slightly discordant, foreign ingredient that must be blended in the dish. In this scene, he overreacts in fear when Dédé's kids play on the wrecking crane. Even during the dance his red clothes stick out visually and he is somewhat

20 This discomfort arises on nearly every occasion the characters find themselves outside of the courtyard. It is worth noting that *Marius et Jeannette* is the only film in Guédiguian's work where no character takes any form of transportation and in which cars have no *raison d'être*.
21 These circular motifs again evokes *Le Crime de Monsieur Lange*.

separated from the others. Later, we see Marius quietly saying goodbye to Jeannette's children at the breakfast table (another meal, and another use of *mise en scène*); a shot the next morning and his place is empty at the same table; and another shot of that evening and his absence is oppressive. But this discord is short-lived, and, like all momentary hints at awful outcomes (for example, when Jeannette looks like she might commit suicide), tragedy is averted and comic resolution re-establishes harmony. In the end, it is once again the group solidarity that saves the couple: Justin and Dédé get drunk with Marius, participate in a slapstick barroom brawl, and get him to admit that, having lost a wife and two children to a car accident, he cannot face the responsibility of a new family.[22] They bring him back to Jeannette's house and tie him to her as she sleeps. As Justin says, he needs '*attachement*': the narrative ends with everyone in love, Justin and Dédé, still drunk, crying out their undying devotion to Caroline and Monique. Friendships overcome vulnerability even as they acknowledge it.

Marius's story involves loss and thus reminds the viewer that, as Powrie notes, 'disappearance and memory ... are key themes of the film', affecting the characters at both the individual and collective level (2001: 139). Taking place in the factory yard, the aioli scene occupies the space that was once the centre of life for the entire neighbourhood. They sit there now, somewhat out of place, watching the past being torn down around them. Caroline complains that the factory should, like Gaudí's buildings (about which Justin has been reading) and the Palais des Papes, be preserved and honoured as a World Heritage site by UNESCO. Jeannette, whose father died from an accident in the same factory, seconds her. But only discussion and friendship can perpetuate that memory in a disconnected, atomised present. This historical context gives another dimension to Marius's story: alone he lives in solitude, with the heavy if unacknowledged memory of loss; with attachment, the strength that comes from friendship, he can admit to his own vulnerability and move on. By filming the factory (as he had already done in *Dernier été*), its demolition and these conversations about it, Guédiguian provides an

---

22 The bar scene echoes Guédiguian's first representations of friendship in *Dernier été*, to the point of including Malek Hamzaoui (who had played *Le Muet*) among the drinkers.

enduring monument to this history, preserving it from inside the community that such spaces have created.

The final scene of the film confirms this memorial intention. Here we see all of the characters walking down a concrete bridge. We watch them from behind, as the actors walk into the frame, as Guédiguian's own voice tells us their sometimes humorous and mainly happy future. Eventually they'll all wind up buried in the cemetery of L'Estaque like 'thousands of workers before them' (and to whom Guédiguian dedicates his film). The ending does point towards the future in what might seem a pessimistic way, figured here in the concrete, post-industrial highway towards which they walk, barring the horizon, perhaps most for the generation of Magali and Malek. According to the voiceover, however, this obstacle is not insurmountable: Magali will become a reporter and Malek a professor of Arabic. But their ability to transition to a changed future will come thanks to the preparation and support they have had in this communist microcosm, thanks to memory.[23]

The film's aesthetic movement has come full circle: out of the detritus of globalisation, the ruined factory, the repetition of the dead-end job, Guédiguian has created a fantastic world, repainted like Jeannette's decrepit kitchen, infused with colour and light. *Marius et Jeannette* could therefore hardly be more different from his work in the 1980s: optimistic where they were pessimistic, utopian where they were dystopian, the film is entirely oriented against working-class tragedy. The overwhelmingly positive reception of the film indicates that the political atmosphere of the period resonated with this vision and that History was perhaps moving again.[24] At the same time, a few

23 Malek, the voiceover explains, will confirm in his studies that Justin's message about religion and tolerance was right; and Magali's journalism will defend the working class. She will write, Guédiguian says, 'les murs des pauvres de L'Estaque sont peints par Cézanne sur des tableaux qui se finissent fatalement sur les murs des riches' (the walls of the poor of L'Estaque are depicted by Cézanne in paintings that end up inevitably on the walls of the rich). This quote ties into a dizzying number of images from Guédiguian's work: his own filming of landscape in L'Estaque since *Dernier été*, the Cézanne poster hanging in Jeannette's kitchen, the expensive reproduction of L'Estaque hanging in the bedroom of a CEO in *À l'attaque!*, etc. In such films, we can see Guédiguian's gesture in the same way: to move into the future with the intention of carving out a space where the social relations of his past find acknowledgement.

24 Derobert and Goudet also noticed that Guédiguian's films seem to run parallel to the 'states of consciousness' of their period: 'Durant les années 80,

critics did find the message too optimistic. At the 1997 Cannes festival, a team of critics from *Les Cahiers du Cinéma* conducted a roundtable discussion in which some of them criticised *Marius et Jeannette* for having failed to 'filmer l'autre, à intégrer l'ennemi, le traître dans votre propre monde' (de Baecque and Toubiana 1997: 59).[25] In an interview with the same journal, Guédiguian rejects the implication that only a traditional realist representation, without comedy or fantasy, could be used to figure capitalism's effects. The *Cahiers* writers were particularly vexed by the light-hearted representation of Dédé, who had once voted for the Front National, for whom they wanted a stronger condemnation. Guédiguian defended the film well: first he cited the percentages of Front National voters in L'Estaque (35 per cent) before explaining that Dédé was not destined to vote Front National and was therefore not an enemy: his vote was a sign of his dimwittedness, and the *philia* of his group shows him the errors of his ways. Guédiguian's slight frustration with these questions may, however, come from the fact that he was doubling down on optimism in his next film, the one he was working on at the time.

À la place du cœur (1998)

For his only adaptation of a literary work, Guédiguian travelled to New York to obtain the rights to one of James Baldwin's later period novels, *If Beale Street Could Talk* (1974), granted, to his surprise, at a fraction of the normal cost by Baldwin's sister. Set in Harlem and the West Village, the book tells the love story of sixteen-year-old Clementine, nicknamed Tish (Clim in the film, played Laure Raoust) and eighteen-year-old Fonny (Bébé in the film, played by Alexandre Ogou), an aspiring sculptor. The two have been close since they were children, and they have always loved each other. However, when they are old enough to marry, and Tish becomes pregnant, Fonny is framed

---

où l'idéologie de l'entreprise domine, vos personnages s'éteignent. Depuis quelques années, la société bouge de nouveau, et vos films, sous l'impulsion souvent de vos héroïnes, deviennent plus positifs' [During the 1980s, when commercial ideology dominated, your characters die at the end. In the past few years, society has begun to move again, and your films, often under the impetus of your female characters, have become more positive.] (Derobert and Goudet 1997: 47).

25 'To film the other, to integrate the enemy or the traitor in your own world.'

by a racist cop for the rape of a Puerto Rican woman, who flees to the island after identifying him in a line-up. Buffeted by her loving family and Fonny's father (Fonny's mother and sisters are religious fanatics who blame Fonny and Tish for causing the situation), Tish continues to work and to fight for Fonny's freedom during her pregnancy. The novel unfolds through a first-person narrative in which Tish tells this story, including her mother Sharon's trip to Puerto Rico to convince Fonny's accuser to retract her testimony. It is easy to see how Baldwin's humanistic valorisation of family bonds, his condemnation of the abuses and weaknesses of the judiciary system, his mystic undertone and the promise of a future represented by the baby would interest Guédiguian, who follows the narrative closely, reproducing the first-person perspective and even much of Baldwin's dialogue.

The move from Baldwin's New York to Guédiguian's Marseilles did require some significant changes, of which three stand out. The first is the representation of race. Baldwin's novel is set in a black universe surrounded by a hostile, white city, whereas most of Guédiguian's characters are white, including Clim and Bébé's parents Franck (Meylan) and Francine (Christine Brücher), who adopted Bébé and his sister when they were infants. The film thus explores less the contours of a 'black' world than the possibilities for racial mixing and integration in a larger 'white', particularly working-class, France. As in the novel, the fathers (Clim's father, Joël Patché is played by Darroussin), along with Clim's mother (Ascaride) and sister, are pleased at the news of Clim's pregnancy. Clim and Bébé also feel at home in a North African restaurant (typical of the quarter of Belsunce, replacing a Spanish restaurant in the Village) and are treated kindly by a landlord who refuses to charge for their apartment while Bébé is in prison. But the film also condemns French racist resistance to multiculturalism, at both a personal and collective level. Bébé's mother, a prudish Catholic, and sister blame the situation on Clim and Bébé's sinfulness rather than the obvious racism. But mostly against them is the racist cop, in an intentionally over-the-top performance by Jacques Pieiller.

One effect of placing Bébé in a white family and making Clim white herself is that Guédiguian can graft their story, through his regular troupe, onto the ever-evolving history of the French working class that Guédiguian knows best. As Joël and Franck's eyes lock at the news of Clim's pregnancy, Clim's voice begins to narrate over a flashback of the men working, Franck on the docks, repairing ship motors (in an echo of the beginning of *Dernier été*) and Joël as a builder. She describes their rise and decline: their satisfaction at supporting families but then the disappearance of satisfying work, their present boredom and humiliation at being replaceable. The baby once again represents hope for a way forward, and in the scene after the announcement that Clim is pregnant the two fathers dance joyfully and drunkenly in a bar, to Louis Armstrong ('Beale Street Blues'), in another archetypical Guédiguian scene. As in the 'contes de L'Estaque' (this film is not billed as one), a non-traditional family is forming out of a dream and out of remnants of two families: two generations will raise the child, two colours of people, a mother, father and at least three grandparents together.

In a second major change, Guédiguian transposed Sharon's trip to Puerto Rico to Sarajevo in the former Yugoslavia, a choice much criticised at the time. In his novel, Baldwin was sensitive to the effects of American imperialism: Sharon discovers in Puerto Rico that society is as divided there as in the USA and that poor people live in even more appalling conditions: 'we are all on the same garbage dump', she declares (Baldwin 2006: 226). In Guédiguian there is a similar expansion of what Rascaroli calls the film's 'scale of spaces', a conscious move on Guédiguian's part:

> to transpose this into the European framework, we thought of the Eastern countries in decline, of Warsaw, Bucharest, and Sarajevo. There, in addition, we had the 'advantage' of a place that was emblematic of communitarian conflicts. It is no longer the spectre of communism haunting Europe, but ethnic war. The worst that could happen to Marseilles would be to turn into Sarajevo.
>
> (Bouzet 1998)

Guédiguian's local cinema here suggests that racism and communitarian conflict is universal. Long documentary-like tracking shots show Madame Patsché's taxi ride from the airport to the city, allowing the viewer to take stock of the ruined state of much of Sarajevo, just a year or two after the Bosnian war of 1992–96 had ended. On her return to Marseilles, she quotes Sharon's declaration: 'nous vivons tous sur le même tas de merde.'[26]

---

26 'But we are on the same garbage dump.'

Guédiguian's third major change to Baldwin's narrative was to integrate it more fully into his utopian and optimistic vision. Clim and Bébé come to form a perfect couple: Guédiguian chose two actors with whom he had never before worked: Laure Raoust and Alexandre Ogou, in part because of their delicate physical beauty. He describes Raoust as a kind of 'Italian virgin' – her ivory skin and large serious eyes give her an angelic quality. Ogou also, with smooth ebony skin, sensitivity, even 'majesty', and his deferential and reverent attitude towards Raoust has his own angelic innocence. In Bébé and Clim's bedroom, outside of the conflicting gazes cast upon them, their bodies have a yin and yang complementarity, very dark and very light, coming together in completion. Their bond also suggests the possibility of a radically different future. Bébé's art almost always represents human forms, nude, free of cultural objects, in one case a baby at the moment of birth. Though this future is in peril, it does not come as a surprise when Madame Patsché seems to have convinced Madame Radic: Bébé's lawyer announces that she will write a letter on his behalf. This is a major contrast with Baldwin's book, which ends on a note of doubt, with Ms Sanchez having become insane and fled to an unknown location in the Puerto Rican hills. Guédiguian ends his film on the reconstitution of the couple: a close-up of Clim in the throes of giving birth is alternated with Bébé chiselling into a new block of marble, about to create another, perhaps a new, human figure. The suggestion of a new future also encompasses the past, the history of the working class. The final shot shows a different block of marble, this one the cornerstone of a building, somewhat in sepia and then out of focus. It is marble perhaps brought from Italy on one of the ships that Franck builds and perhaps set in place by Joël or someone like him. It is fading but new; fresh people are walking past it towards the future.

The image of the cornerstone resonates with an important new stylistic effect that Guédiguian uses here and that he will exploit later. In one short scene, at the moment Bébé asks for Clim's hand, Clim's father (Darroussin) has a momentary daydream from the past about his wife (Ascaride). We see the two actors in the flower of youth: Darroussin watches Ascaride sleep and slowly pulls the sheets down revealing her young, nude body. The images are taken from *Ki lo sa?*, made some seventeen years earlier. Note that Clim is sixteen or seventeen in this film, so that the dream could plausibly evoke the night of her conception. This technique is particularly effective here for three reasons. First, it suggests continuity: Bébé and Clim's story is attached to a history, and here that history receives a uniquely cinematic anchoring in time. Secondly, the shot rewrites the pessimism of the earlier film. In *Ki lo sa?* Darroussin was a voyeur, uncovering Ascaride as she sleeps, only to be rejected when she awakens. Here it has precisely the opposite function, as the beginning of a love story that will continue into another generation. This opens up Guédiguian's films to revision and play. Finally, and most importantly, this very original effect owes its existence to something larger than individual films, a stubborn dedication to working with friends, and it thus points directly outside of the particular narrative towards the larger project. (I will return to this point in the Conclusion.)

Guédiguian filmed *À la place du cœur* in the summer of 1997, after the screening of *Marius et Jeannette* at Cannes but before its commercial release. The film was therefore made by a still relatively unknown film-maker but received as the follow-up to one of the most viewed and debated films of the previous year. Expectations were high, and, according to the majority of critical appraisals, the film fell short. Didier Péron's review in *Libération* is a typical if vociferous critique, denouncing Guédiguian's willingness to 'take on the burden of every Manichean sin of the genre': the bad fascist, the Catholic prude and the hero worship of the workers. In the end, Péron accuses the film of 'infantilising' the viewer and giving a representation of the people as children or as 'dead-eyed taxidermy specimens'.[27]

Some of Péron's and others' criticisms may be exaggerated, but they are generally aimed at central elements in the film and really in most of Guédiguian's work since *L'Argent fait le bonheur*. Many, such as Phil Powrie, had tolerated the sentimentality of *Marius et Jeannette* in part because of the Brechtian distanciation (Powrie 2001: 142), but this film is much more sentimental, less self-conscious, less playful in style, more exalted and assured that small-group solidarity could overcome a broad societal problem. Its characters' goodness wins out perhaps too easily in a way that viewers could not easily recognise as

27 A minority of influential critics have defended the film: Louis Skorecki in 2003 compared Guédiguian to Fassbinder and Sirk for his ability to 'wrestle through the crossroads of melodrama' and combine the 'unreal and the intimate' (Skorecki 1999); whereas Jean-Michel Frodon is sympathetic but thinks that only Guédiguian should be working in this vein (Frodon 1998).

a possibility in their own lives. In response, Guédiguian reiterates that he was not seeking realism and that he was pushing a melodramatic genre as far as he could. Though he did not renounce this film, his follow-up did unveil a greater variety of tone and narrative technique, partially in self-critique and partially in response to others.

À l'attaque (2000)

À l'attaque returns to the genre of the *conte de L'Estaque*, but this time the primary narrative is accompanied with a self-conscious narrative frame: in the manner of Julien Duvivier's *La Fête à Henriette* (1951), two writers (and friends) of different temperaments (Yvan and Xavier, also the film's director), set out to write the screenplay of a 'political' film in which they will represent the conflict between 'rich and poor'. As Guédiguian says in the press release about the film, 'their digressions, quarrels, and reconciliations will interfere non-stop with the exemplary story of the Moliterno and Co. garage'. This set-up gives Guédiguian frequent opportunity to explore narrative and aesthetic choices, defending some while rejecting others.

The primary narrative, beginning with a typical panning shot over L'Estaque, again with the chirruping sound of cicadas, reunites the core group of actors back in familiar territory. The Moliternos resemble the loose family of *Marius et Jeannette*, with three generations living together above the family's auto-repair garage, including childhood friend Jean-Do (Darroussin), who is not related by blood but whose wife has left him and who is now in love with the widow Lola (Ascaride), the daughter of grandpa Moliterno (Boudet) and sister of Gigi (Meylan). Present also are: Malud, a young African-origin street vendor with hopes of becoming a lawyer; his friend Vanessa (Pesenti), who sells flowers; and the lazy Henri, who represents, according to the writers, 'the right to refuse to work'. The film-makers insert this boisterous and stressed 'family' into a very precisely outlined economic problem: the family owes back payments on their mortgage because they are waiting for their primary customer, a large multinational shipping company, to pay them for previously rendered services. The president of the company, M. Moreau (Banderet), decides to move his affiliate overseas for cheap labour and default on the company's debts. As financial ruin looms, Jean-Do (Darroussin) and

Gigi (Meylan) break into Moreau's house at night (attempting to steal a reproduction of a Braque painting of L'Estaque, in illustration of Magali's quote in *Marius et Jeannette*), but they are clumsy and are arrested. The women in the family manage to lure Moreau into a car (using sexy Vanessa as bait) and kidnap him: the grandfather, a former Italian partisan, holds a gun to his head. Malud informs the media, who come to film their demands. The entire city turns out to see the stand-off, which ends in success for the family. It is an unrealistic narrative about micro-revolutionary action dealing with the real problems of debt and cynical corporate irresponsibility.

What makes the film different is the constant back and forth between the two film-makers and the diegesis of their film. It begins with an animated theatre curtain that opens onto credits and the two writers beginning their work. These characters (Denis Podalydès and Jacques Pieiller), played by actors outside of Guédiguian's core group (though Pieiller may be somewhat familiar as Otto in *À la vie, à la mort!* and the cop in *À la place du cœur*), come as an intrusion of a 'realistic' space into the fable space, presented as a product of their imaginations. Sometimes the characters are left stuttering on screen while a cut back to the writers shows them arguing over a line of dialogue. They type a line, and a cut back to the film shows a character saying it. At one moment, an actress played by Pascale Roberts must break character to directly ask the writers what she should do: she is on screen but her role is not yet written. Many scenes allow the writers to explore purely comic digressions. At one moment of distraction the writers imagine a scene in the 'enchanted whorehouse'. Picking up on a word play from Jacques Demy ('le bordel *en*-chanté'), the scene is sung as a musical comedy, though with a number of vulgar puns, such as 'pretty fairy, fairy fellations' ('de jolies fées, fées, fellations!'). But it is also shown to be just a scene: at the end, the image becomes flat; the screen is transformed into a sheet of paper that one of the writers crumples up and throws away.[28]

These scenes tell not only the story of the film but also the story of how to tell the story. The authorial intrusions clarify once and for all that Guédiguian is not interested in realism and that to read his films as lacking in subtlety, too nostalgic or unrealistic means to miss that

---

28 See Ousselin (2007) for a fairly exhaustive account of these authorial incursions.

they are what O'Shaughnessy calls 'fables of the possible' (2008: 59). The director in the film argues that the film needs only to be attached to plausibility by a mere thread for the film is written for those who still have a 'wish for a dream'. In this way, the film answers the critics of *À la place du cœur*: at the end of the film, the two writers sit in the corner of an auditorium waiting for the announcement of an award for best screenplay. They of course do not win, and when Yvan blames the loss on too much 'Manichaeism', Xavier replies in the blunt and comic manner of the characters, with a Marseillais 'va te faire enculer!'[29]

But the film can also be read as a self-critique. Without disavowing the political fable of the *conte de L'Estaque*, the conceit allows Guédiguian to suggest, perhaps most of all to himself, that each film is a product of choices that could have taken many other turns. One shift in tone stands out from the others. Once Lola finishes her impassioned plea on the television, she picks up the crying baby and opens the shutters. Shockingly, a policeman's bullet rips through her, and, as she turns to the others, falling with the crying baby in her arms, the grandfather responds by putting another bullet through the head of the corporate boss. The scene, removed by the older Xavier, stands in stark contrast with the 'actual' finale with which they quickly replace it in which the boss writes them a cheque and Lola stands at the window with it, in front of a throng of cheering people. Given the number of arbitrary changes in direction that the film takes and the presence of this brutal scene in the mind of the viewer, this happy ending has a frail, less confident quality: good sentiments may not be enough, and a mere thread separates utopia and dystopia; the *conte de L'Estaque* can turn into tragedy in a moment, as it would in Guédiguian's next film.

References

Baldwin, James (2006) *If Beale Street Could Talk*, New York: Vintage.
Bazin, André (1986) *Jean Renoir*, New York: Simon & Schuster.
Bloch, Ernst (1995) *The Principle of Hope*, vol. I, Cambridge, Mass.: MIT Press.
Bouzet, Ange-Dominique (1998) 'Robert Guédiguian défend son approche poétique: "Je veux me situer dans l'excès"', *Libération*, 9 December,

[29] 'Go bugger yourself!'

available at http://next.liberation.fr/culture/1998/12/09/robert-guediguian-defend-son-approche-poetique-je-veux-me-situer-dans-l-exces_255493 (accessed 2 January 2016).

Brecht, Bertolt (1992) 'A Short Organum for the Theatre', *Brecht on Theatre: The Development of an Aesthetic*, trans. John Willet, New York: Hill & Wang, pp. 179–205.

Danel, Isabelle (2008) *Conversation avec Robert Guédiguian*, Paris: Les Carnets de l'Info.

Derobert, Eric and Stéphane Goudet (1997) 'Entretien avec Robert Guédiguian "Intervenir dans le monde, plutôt que dans l'histoire du cinema"', *Positif*, 442, 42–8.

De Baecque, Antoine and Serge Toubiana (1997) 'Le Goût de L'Estaque: Entretien avec Robert Guédiguian', *Cahiers du Cinéma*, 518, 58–61.

Frodon, Jean-Michel (1998) '*À la place du cœur*', *Le Monde*, 10 December.

Guédiguian, Robert (2000) Note accompanying press release of *À l'attaque*.

Ouesselin, Edward (2007) 'Un conte politisé: *À l'attaque!* de Robert Guédiguian', *The French Review*, 81:1, 124–34.

Péron, Didier (1998) 'Dans *À la place du cœur* ... tous les clichés du film social ...', *Libération*, 9 December, available at http://next.liberation.fr/culture/1998/12/09/dans-a-la-place-du-coeur-le-realisateur-de-marius-et-jeannette-reprend-tous-les-cliches-du-film-soci_255491 (accessed 2 January 2016).

Rascaroli, Laura (2006) 'The Place of the Heart: Scaling Spaces in Robert Guédiguian's Cinema', *Studies in French Cinema*, 6:2, 95–105.

Sahuc, Stéphane (2011) *Parlons politique: Maryse Dumas – Robert Guédiguian*, Paris: Les Éditions Arcane-17.

Skorecki, Louis (1999) 'Entre Fassbinder et Cocteau: les excès magnifiques d'*À la place du cœur*', *Libération*, 9 December.

Standing, Guy (2011) *The Precariat*, London: Bloomsbury Academic.

O'Shaughnessy, Martin (2008) *The New Face of Political Cinema*, New York: Berghahn Books.

Powrie, Phil (1999) 'Heritage, History, and "New Realism": French Cinema in the 1990s', in Phil Powrie (ed.), *French Cinema in the 1990s: Continuity and Difference*, Oxford: Oxford University Press, pp. 1–21.

—— (2001) '*Marius et Jeannette*: Nostalgia and Utopia', in Lucy Mazdon (ed.), *France on Film: Reflections on Popular French Cinema*, London: Wallflower, pp. 133–44.

Ungar, Steven (2000) '*Marius et Jeannette*: A Political Tale', *IRIS*, 29: spring, 39–52.

1 Gérard Meylan as Gilbert in *Dernier été*

2 Ariane Ascaride in *Au fil d'Ariane*

3 Jean-Pierre Darroussin in his taxi in *La Ville est tranquille*

4 Gérard Meylan and Ariane Ascaride in *Dernier été*

5 Gérard Meylan, Ariane Ascaride, Jean-Pierre Darroussin and Pierre Banderet in *Ki lo sa?*

6 The meal at the end of *À la vie, à la mort!*

7 Ariane Ascaride, Pascale Roberts and Frédérique Bonnal in the courtyard in *Marius et Jeannette*

8 The Caronte Viaduct in *Dieu vomit les tièdes*

9 The beach ball and L'Estaque

10 The demolition of the factory

4

Themes and variation
Films since 2000

The 1990s were a period of great optimism for Guédiguian, but, as they came to an end, there were indications that History would not fulfil its promises so easily. At the same time, Guédiguian did not revert to the pessimism of the 1980s: he did not reject the *conte de L'Estaque*, nor renounce the desire to re-enchant the world. Moving forward into the 2000s, the basic project of 'living with friends' was the backbone of his work, and the friends still measured their project against an ideal of History in mutation. They did not always come out on top, but they continued to search for zones of utopia and resistance in a larger variety of narrative situations.

To examine the nine films released since 2000, I will divide this chapter into three parts. In the first set of films, Guédiguian deepened his study of the family, as *philia*, in new generic and tonal settings ranging from dystopia to utopia: these films examined violence, sexuality and political commitment in a broader range of spaces than those set in the microcosm of L'Estaque. The second group of films took Guédiguian even farther afield, sometimes because the films themselves were commissioned or originated in ideas developed by someone else. In these films, Guédiguian explored the historical genre and, through it, national or ethnic identity, though *philia* is still the benchmark by which one judges their characters' actions. Finally, tweaking the chronology just slightly by including *Lady Jane* (2008) with later films, the last section returns more explicitly to Guédiguian's long-term project and closer to his geographical origin. Each of these films deconstructed a figure of human relations – the masks of revenge, self-satisfaction or bourgeois complacency – to locate a more open, ethical model of human relationship. My goal in this chapter is, as far as is possible, to avoid repetition of ideas discussed through earlier works while indicating what is new or deepened in each film.

Dystopia/Utopia: the family as *philia*

La Ville est tranquille (2001)

La Ville est tranquille, written and filmed at the same time as *À l'Attaque!*, is an example of Guédiguian's willingness to explore generic and emotional territories far removed from fables and optimism. The film starts off prettily enough with lavender cursive credits over white screens and then Satie's calm *gymnopédies* over a long, slow panning shot of Marseilles, from the outskirts to the old port, with images of beautiful buildings, the basilica and a number of pleasure ships included, a shot that, Thomas Sotinel writes, 'resembles a post card' (*tient de la carte postale*) and that might evoke the types of 'pretty images' for which *À la place du cœur* was criticised (Sotinel 2001). At the same time, the sweeping shot presents Marseilles in a panoptical view in which no humans or small-scale habitations are present. There are also already signs that this calm image will be contradicted. As Philip Anderson has argued, the music quickly jumps from one melody to another and becomes 'increasingly difficult to rationalise as mood music', suggesting an ironic pastiche, especially over this long camera movement (2008: 238).

In notes accompanying the film, Guédiguian refers to a false sense of calm that Marseilles can sometimes emanate:

> one has the impression that the city has laid itself out as if to rest after the day's hard work ... The sun meets the sea and one can imagine tons of lovely scenes ... People have returned home and are dining, telling stories, celebrating their birthdays ... I've always felt that this serenity was just an appearance, and that evil, dangerous, fearful forces were at work, which could torch the city at any moment.[1]

Here Guédiguian refers directly to families and domestic situations threatened by forces of evil, which will turn out, as Anderson has

[1] See press materials accompanying the film.

noted, to be the familiar forces of the closure of history and the demise of social solidarity. The film takes place in a number of different 'homes', set in different social milieus and in different generations but all undergoing forces that threaten to destroy the relationships within them. The film also considers the relationship among the various families and homes in order to locate, if possible, any cohesion in the collective fauna of the city. Unlike *Marius et Jeannette* or *À la place du cœur*, *La Ville est tranquille* returns to an 'apocalyptic' view of history (again, see Anderson), though I will also suggest a tempering of this pessimism.

The most desolate household of the film belongs to Michèle (Ascaride), a fish-packing factory worker, entering middle age, who has lost her first love (this could not survive a messy illegal abortion when she was fourteen) and who is now married to a long-term unemployed alcoholic (Banderet) and lives in an enormous housing project. Michèle's daughter Fiona (Julie-Marie Parmentier) is hopelessly addicted to drugs, sells her body to pay for her habit and has just had a child of her own by some unknown father. Michèle struggles to work, take care of baby Ameline and Fiona, with no help from her husband, who has grown increasingly bitter and reactionary and who has joined a right-wing political party, the Préférence Nationale. The cross-editing of Michèle preparing baby formula with shots of her preparing the cocaine for her daughter emphasise Fiona's regression: she is nearly always in bed, sobbing uncontrollably. This impossible-to-sustain situation overwhelms Michèle, and she finally gives her daughter the fatal overdose that was certain to come at some point anyway.

The film's second failed home is set in a much wealthier social milieu and is associated with Marseilles's historical situation. Yves and Viviane Froment belong to the city's political and economic elite: Yves is an architect and urban designer while Viviane donates her time to teach dance to prisoners and handicapped youth. But the social idealism of their youth has given way to cynicism, especially in Yves, who now participates in transforming Marseilles from a working city into a pleasure port, filled with monuments and cruise ships, the postcard Marseilles evoked by the opening camera sweep. Viviane is disillusioned with her husband, in whom she recognises a desire for power, seen in his willingness to work with the extreme right and his incessant attempts to seduce younger women. At the same time, she benefits from the marble-walled bathroom of their apartment and the stylish dinners that unite the political left and right on the rooftop terraces of the *Vieux Port*. She begins an affair with an idealistic young man of African origins, Abderramane, played by Alexandre Ogou (Bébé from *À la place du cœur*).

Besides a very brief exchange between Michèle and Viviane at the height of their suffering, and a chance encounter between Abderramane and Michèle and Fiona, there is no real narrative connection between these two failed families. The film places them most frequently in their own bourgeois apartments, the least communal of Guédiguian's living spaces, as Rascaroli has pointed out (2006: 99). The only quality shared by the characters is that they are all isolated by an insidious operation of history. Looking at the port of Marseilles or in the taxi with his wife, Yves comments that History has ended (a now familiar discourse): he sees himself creating the Marseilles of the future, based on making money. But the film shows us the other side of the coin, the history that continues after the end of History, of people that fall into unemployment like Michèle's husband, underemployment like herself, drug use like her daughter, prison like Abderramane. The narrative lines cross only in that they occupy the same exhausted historical moment.

The film insists on particularly French social divisions, especially racial divisions. From one point of view, the relationship between Viviane and Abderramane indicates, as in *À la place du cœur*, an attempt to overcome racial difference. Out of prison, Abderramane devotes his life to raising awareness and helping Viviane with her volunteer work. When they make love, as in *À la place du cœur*, their contrasting skin colours form a rather simplistic representation of racism overcome by love: in a generally positive review, Serge Kaganski calls it 'un cliché à la Benetton' (2001: 39). And yet the film deconstructs this cliché. It first gestures briefly to a different potential love story between Abderramane and Fiona (who resembles Clim in the earlier film): this storyline seems more valuable since Abderramane could help Fiona with more serious problems than upper-middle-class guilt, but it is one more missed connection and they never meet again. More tragically, one of the Préférence Nationale friends (played by Lenglet), hoping to scare some kids of colour who walk by as they are putting up political posters one night, accidently murders Abderramane.[2] (The men flee the scene.) Towards the end of the film, Viviane comes to the housing project for Abderramane's funeral service. We learn that this is the first time she has been there: she asks directions to his building from Michèle, who happens to be calling the police after the death of her daughter. (The two only meet in death, and then randomly.) Viviane finally arrives during a Muslim ritual from which she is excluded by what Kaganski calls the 'mur invisible' (invisible wall) of her fear to cross the threshold. The camera, fixed and located outside the apartment, looking over her shoulder, uses the multiple frames of the image and the doorway to imply distance: her Benetton moment was a mirage.

There is also no counter-discourse of solidarity in the film. Paul (Darroussin), a dockworker and union organiser, abandons his striking co-workers and accepts a lay-off incentive, with which he puts a down payment on a luxurious taxi. Paul stands in strong contrast to his parents, played by Boudet and Roberts, often the moral and political anchors of Guédiguian's films. Their small house, in L'Estaque rather than the city centre, with its brighter colours, wind-blown geraniums, a softer light and children giggling on the other side of the green woven fence of their terrace, belongs to another time, the mythical past of a class identity. Paul's father expresses how far solidarity has sunk as he inspects his son's taxi: 'Just ten or fifteen years ago, what you did there, dropping the comrades, I would have been the first to spit in your face; but today ... most of them vote extreme right anyway.' While he speaks, the camera roams around the interior where we read the 'price to pay' of the meter. Paul also tells him how to adjust the rear-view mirrors in a way that seems more about the past than about the road: his father cannot seem to make the buttons work and keeps locking the doors. A scene or two later, Yves Froment, bickering with his wife in the back of this same taxi, says that 'history is finished' and 'there is nothing to look forward to except maybe getting used to it.' The scene is typical of a tension in the camera's frames, reflecting the superficial brushing together of stories. The camera moves forward and backward, but Paul here is but an anonymous 'monsieur' before whom they air their intimate disputes and who charges seventy francs in the end. Paul's solitude also enters his

---

2 This scene tracks the erosion of political solidarity from a similar one in *Rouge midi*, where workers humiliate some fascist poster hangers.

sexual life: the walls of his apartment are covered in porn centrefolds; he frequently visits the prostitutes who gather under the highway overpass; and he lies to his mother about finding a partner.

La Ville est tranquille is a film of bodies, at their most physical, over which the characters have lost control. Fiona is in a constant state of need, and Parmentier (during the same year as her similarly physical role in *Les Blessures assassins*) gives a punishing performance: constantly sweating and trembling, her crying and the baby's crying are loud and resemble each other, often to the point of serious discomfort for the viewer. Michèle's loss of agency is represented with particular intensity through her hands. In the first scene, her hands are freezing cold because of the work she does, and the film lingers on her as she tries to warm them up by blowing on them. Later, we see her hands in close-up, instinctively warming up the baby's bottle. The decision to kill her daughter is shown through an elegant close-up of her hands emptying not the normal single bag of cocaine into the spoon but several. She also loses control over her body: in one scene, Michèle, dressed as usual in a constrictive miniskirt, is returning from buying drugs for her daughter and encounters a police checkpoint. She quickly turns her moped in another direction, but falls and tries clumsily to pick it up as its wheels turn. In another scene, she tries to become a prostitute to buy her daughter's drugs: she gets drunk and wanders around trying to find a client before tumbling to the ground, the shaking camera reflecting her lack of balance. Body and mind are separated in each of these scenes: the impulse for action comes not from persons making rational decisions but from a social and historically driven desperation.[3]

Through the final main character, Gérard (Meylan), Guédiguian suggests a more conscious link to a lost past. Like Paul's parents, Gérard seems to belong to a previous world, far away from the city and its housing projects. The film flashes back twice to Gérard and Michèle's past. In the first (the second takes place at the end of the

[3] More than in Guédiguian's other films, economic forces turn women's bodies into commodities. Early in the film, when Paul stops to see the prostitutes to show off his new taxi, he tells them that he cannot have sex with them in the car because it is his 'work tool', to which one of the prostitutes responds 'and me, that's a work tool too' ('et moi, c'est un outil de travail'). This is the ultimate in economic exploitation, but also a treatment of prostitutes as workers and dignified human beings.

film), they are children, already in love (like Clim and Bébé in *À la place du cœur*), running around the bar that Gérard, refusing to give up the past, now owns as an adult. But a botched illegal abortion when Michèle was fourteen tore their relationship apart. Fiona's death repeats this first lost child. Gérard's association with the tragic illegal abortion makes even stranger his liaison not only with Ameline, a highly sensual girl who looks like a young Michèle but also with a right-wing anti-abortion activist, given to fascistic myths of the French as a 'people of life'. Gérard feels an insatiable desire for her even though he loathes her political convictions: he is another figure of solitude.

Gérard, somewhat like Frisé in *Dieu vomit les tièdes*, is violent. First he is connected to the murky criminal character René, who also has a connection to Paul's father, forged while fighting together in the Resistance against the Nazi occupation. René hires, or assigns, Gérard to assassinate a local politician. We do not know the motivation, but we can assess the political interpretation that the act receives from Paul's father, who reads about it in the newspaper. He is less disturbed by the killing than by the fact that the victim, a left-wing politician, was in attendance at a party at the home of an extreme right-wing politician, with Ameline too, the daughter of another right-winger. He concludes that politicians now see the people as a 'flock of sheep' and vows bitterly never to vote again. To hear Boudet pronounce this, after his roles as repository of a memory of resistance in *À la vie, à la mort!* and so many other films, adds to the film's sense of historical despair. Gérard seems to agree with him: as he scans the party through the cross hairs of his rifle, he focuses on several attendees, searching for his victim, but one has the impression that he could shoot any of them equally well, including Ameline. His violence is political, but nihilistic, without the ethical dimension of the Resistance or really any ideological content.

A pessimistic reading of the film is supported by Gérard's last act of violence: after helping Michèle cover up the killing of her daughter, he drives slowly along the highway, inside the car rather than outside as in the camera sweep of the film's beginning, listening to Janis Joplin (a soundtrack that cost Guédiguian a significant part of his budget but which evokes the passion, pain and impending doom of the characters). He stops at a crosswalk where a young man (Yann Trégouët) steps in front of the car to taunt him. Gérard steps out of the car as the young man taunts him, pulls a gun and jams it into the younger man's mouth. The scene is quite complex: the young man, with his long hair and band of friends, resembles Meylan's younger self in *Dernier été*. As Gérard contemplates shooting the kid, the camera cuts to the second flashback of Gérard and Michèle, this one recycled from the end of *Dernier été*: Meylan and Ascaride walk down into the litter-strewn *crique* and kiss. When the shot returns to the present, Gérard has a change of mind, puts the gun in his own mouth and pulls the trigger. It is a shot that comes right out of the 'alternative ending' of *À l'attaque!*, brutal and unexpected, but this time without any authorial intervention to set things back in order. This act of desperation has as little personal explanation, beyond this flashback, as Michèle's dealing out of Fiona's overdose. The characters kill or self-destruct seemingly because, at this juncture in history, it is better for them not to continue. This seems to reflect Philip Anderson's 'apocalyptic' interpretation of violence in Guédiguian's work as a sign that the characters are 'metonymies of the present within an historical process', at a period coming to a close, that of the 'agony of a social class' (2008: 243, 240). One might suspect that Guédiguian has returned to the grim depiction of history he had supposedly exorcised in *Dieu vomit les tièdes*.

At the same time, there are a few elements in the film that assert a less nihilistic vision, as in the relationship between Paul and Michèle. It starts when Paul stops to help Michèle whose moped has broken down. It continues after the scene in which Michèle tries to become a prostitute, in what Kaganski has called a '*scène d'anthologie*' (an anthology piece). As a drunk Michèle lies on the pavement, an arm reaches into the high-angle frame to help her up: Paul. He gives her 300 francs and a ride. In the taxi, he tells her about himself (exaggerating his success as he does with his parents) and about how he left the docks for his current life. He is trying to strike a disillusioned attitude but admits that it wasn't easy given the union and all the 'tra-la-la' of solidarity. Michèle begins to weep. He then demonstrates just how strongly his belief in solidarity had once been. First he sings the International (with 'some verses which there aren't many who know the words'). He then sings it in English, Italian, German and Russian, slowly coaxing a smile out of Michèle: the camera keeps shifting back and forth, in shots that succeed in linking the characters more than was possible in the scene in the taxi with the Froment couple.

This is, of course, a highly ambiguous scene: Paul is faking success (he will lose the taxi because of debt), and the scene will end with Michèle unlocking her moped to go to buy more drugs for her daughter. Paul will also return to Michèle, this time to pay for sex. But they also develop a more human relationship that makes the monetary transactions awkward: Paul's interest in Michèle's hopes for her granddaughter are juxtaposed awkwardly with his payment to her as she straightens her skirt after sex in the car: perhaps he even uses the sex as a pretext to help her financially. These scenes rewrite the meaning that the viewer takes from the taxi: this symbol of working-class treason and contemporary loneliness still seems haunted by a solidarity seeking to take form, and perhaps a new friendship. When Paul stops by Michèle's house at the end, just after Gérard has helped her make Fiona's death look like a suicide, Gérard encourages him to stay behind and help Michèle as best he can. The film poses the question of which opposing tendency will win out: the solitude of history or the fleeting connections that might develop into stronger relationships.

The ending implies that creative approaches might help to regenerate a sense of community in dire times. In an extremely well-timed shot, just as Gérard pulls the trigger of his gun, sending a fountain of brains from the top of his head, the camera performs another sweep across the street to a piano delivery truck moving in the opposite direction. There is no causality between the shooting and the delivery, but they again happen simultaneously and in the same space. Michèle's husband and two co-workers, including the one who killed Abderramane, drive to L'Estaque to deliver a grand piano to the home of Sarkis, the young Georgian immigrant who was playing Satie at beginning of the film, to raise money to buy an instrument. Sarkis plays Bach this time, and deftly, his fingers driven by his talent and hard work, not by his tragic history. As he plays in the sunken courtyard where he lives, his father looks on approvingly, family and neighbours gather around to listen, and the camera pans up to walkways elevated over the courtyard to show dozens of them, of all colours and origins, the first communal space of the film. The right-wingers are there too, but the presence of the many others suggests at least one collective possibility. But these encounters must still be developed into relationships rather than reverting to solitude, meaning in history must be created, and people must reassert control over their destinies.

Marie-Jo et ses deux amours (2002)

Marie-Jo et ses deux amours is, as its title hints, a film about infidelity, a surprisingly individualistic, apolitical and even bourgeois theme for a film-maker like Guédiguian. It seems like a banal story: Marie-Jo is nearing middle age; her life is devoted to serving others (she is driver and in-home aid to sick people and does accounts for her husband, Daniel [Darroussin]); her daughter is graduating from the *lycée* and entering the university. Though nothing is wrong with her marriage (she loves her husband), she meets Marco (Meylan) with whom she also falls in love. The film is split between two couples, two homes. First there is Daniel's construction business, which resembles somewhat the Moliterno garage, where Marie-Jo does the books, though here the home business is lonelier, without the comings and goings of friends and community members. The second home is Marco's apartment, nestled under the tiled roofs and with a view of the Panier neighbourhood, a romantic nest. People are separate, as befits the alienated bourgeois love story. But Marie-Jo attempts to bridge a distance; indeed, she loves both men and cannot bring herself to abandon either for the other. Underneath the bourgeois tragedy one thus finds something entirely different: a desire for a sexual utopia.

The film delves deeply into a theme found throughout Guédiguian's previous work: the representation of sex. Many of Guédiguian's films condemn the sexual commodification of a capitalistic society, most recently in *La Ville est tranquille*. Some of his films also represent sex as embroiled in power relations (as when Marie-Sol is attacked by her boss in *À la vie, à la mort*), or in conflicts or jealousies within a class (like Maggiorina as the trophy of the Gilbert/Boule fight in *Dernier été*). There have also been counter-figures as well: the humanity with which prostitutes are treated, despite their exploitation, in *À la vie, à la mort* or *La Ville est tranquille*. Other women have asserted their sexual freedom or resisted traditional gender roles: Maggiorina's refusal to marry the barber in *Rouge midi*, the coupling of the priest and Simona Viala in *L'Argent fait le bonheur*, for example. Sexual relationships do not conform to societal norms in relation to demographics either, as can be seen in the emphasised colour difference between Clim and Bébé in *À la place du cœur*, or the representation of sex among older people in *Marius et Jeannette*; there are also erotic or love relationships between children, such as Bébé and Clim in *À la place du cœur*. Orientation is nearly exclusively heterosexual in Guédiguian's films, though *Dernier été* contains a criticism of homophobia. In general, Guédiguian's films condemn power as it functions through sex and loosens societal strictures.

These representations of sex are in part due to ideological commitments. In one scene from *Rouge midi*, Pierre and his girlfriend Céline are shown lying naked in a grassy spot. They are framed horizontally in full shot, glowing in soft rays of sunlight, giggling, when Pierre describes the opening of William Morris's *News from Nowhere*, in which a man wakes up one morning to find himself in a future without money or serious conflict, the communist utopia. Pierre and Céline illustrate Morris's image of sexual utopia, lacking in shame, based on equality between men and women, interested in entire beings and not in the eroticising of women's bodies (the camera focuses primarily on Pierre's body), in a pastoral setting outside bourgeois society.

Morris was strongly influenced by Friedrich Engels' *The Origin of the Family, Private Property and the State*. For Engels, family structure, closely related to the production of life, follows the course of the materialist view of history. The present configuration of the family would, according to this theory, be related to the rise of capitalism: 'the arrival of the capitalist mode of production – with its division of labour and private property – dictated the development of the monogamian family, and fundamental to that was a system of inheritance from fathers to children' (Hunt in Engels 2010: 10). *News from Nowhere*, serialised in 1890, six years after Engels' text, can be seen as a utopian image of post-Revolution inter-gender relationships. Back on the grass in *Rouge midi*, Pierre could also have mentioned the friend of the narrator of *News from Nowhere*, Dick, and his spouse Clara. Clara has in fact separated from Dick to live with another man, but, because there is no private property, the crisis of their relationship does not lead to attendant problems involving divorce courts and money. She is not condemned on moral grounds and is free to chose whomever she wants to live with, since marriage is a 'contract of passion or sentiment' and impossible to force (Morris 1993: 91).

In love with two men, Marie-Jo is in contradiction with her bourgeois lifestyle, but she is also attuned to a utopian desire for another arrangement based on freedom. Perhaps the most original element of this film is how it explores this desire in the very bodies of the actors, especially in a dozen or so scenes in which they appear naked. At these moments, the viewer is not presented with hot young bodies framed in pornographic poses. These older bodies, however, are still filmed erotically, shown as beautiful, dignified in spite of age, in 'havens of peace' as Kantcheff expresses it (2013: 164). The first shot of Ascaride in her bedroom, dressed in understated underclothing, lightly made up and softly lit, has her framed from the knees up in an elegant vertical frame made up of a mirror surrounded by her dark bedroom. We also see Ascaride inclined on the beach, the sun glistening in the water on her face and arms. Marco's apartment and the house are both set up in ways that allow the lovers to stand naked in the doorway with soft natural light illuminating their bodies. Special attention to lighting also emphasises the actors' skin in close-ups in dark bedrooms. The actors are comfortable being filmed naked: in one scene, Darroussin stands drinking rosé from a bottle, naked, framed by a doorway. His body is clearly ageing, but he appears completely comfortable and at home in soft, early morning light. In Meylan's case, this level of comfort was attained after several months visiting nudist colonies: Meylan mentions that his nearly grown children had never seen him nude, but that he had grown so comfortable that he would have liked to see Guédiguian push his work on the nude even further.

When these bodies do come together in sex, the film does not suggest commodification, exchange or instant gratification but rather affection and a link of love. Bodies are not on display except when people share them with each other. At the most intense moments of sex Guédiguian will focus on the characters' faces, horizontal and in profile, staring into each other's eyes (once in Marco's bedroom, the first time we see them together; and once under the tarp covering the boat that Daniel bought her for her birthday). Close-ups show a hand touching an arm or a leg, or the caress of a back. There are also repeated shots of the lovers in bed afterwards, an arm around each other or Marco simply thanking Marie-Jo. Sex is intense but also other-oriented. At the same time, sex and nudity take place away from other characters, away from society, in a utopian setting, often lit up in the Mediterranean light. Sex is a part of openness and connection to the other, an integral part of a story, a link that Marie-Jo desires to prolong and deepen.[4]

The conflict of having a lover and a husband is inscribed in the *mise en scène* of body as it emerges from the intimate utopian space and must join society again. In one scene, Marie-Jo is putting her clothes back on after an afternoon with Marco, who, in sadness, reproaches her for leaving him for her 'comfortable' situation. Suddenly tears come to her eyes as she stands wearing a blouse but naked from the waist down, an awkwardness that reflects her situation. A similar shot echoes this one later when, after making love with Daniel, she sits uncomfortably on the floor, nude, explaining the same thing to him as he sleeps. Another scene of Marie-Jo and Marco in bed ends with the arrival of her daughter Julie who has stopped by to pick up a notebook from Marco. When Marco shows her out, after a cup of coffee, we hear Marie-Jo weeping and find her cowering naked in the corner of the bedroom. There is a related technique in the editing, which must articulate the distance between sets of people in different places as one of Marie-Jo's lives continually disrupts the other. One of Marie-Jo's afternoons with Marco takes her away from home on a day when Julie and her boyfriend, Sylvain, learn whether they have passed their *baccalauréat*. The trip to the school, with Daniel in the truck with Julie, is cut with a lovemaking scene long enough to make us forget what is happening in the 'other life' until we cut back to it several minutes later. Such uneven parallel editing underscores Marie-Jo's incapacity to live fully in all of her narratives and in all of her homes simultaneously.[5]

4 These utopian representations of sex are accompanied by a more in-depth work on the image generally, especially through colours and filters, in collaboration with a rare newcomer, the director of photography Renato Berta. The visual beauty of the bodies in love pours over into a representation of the landscape as well: Berta mentions shooting one scene at five in the morning in order to get blues and the reflections of the sunrise on the rocks, which are filmed in the same colours and light as the bodies themselves.
5 We see such incursions on both sides, and it is underlined by sound editing and frame composition as well. When Daniel buys Marie-Jo a boat for her birthday, she gets a phone call from Marco who wants to sing 'Happy Birthday'

The film's narrative is most fully invested in representing the characters' sexuality, but suggestions of dissatisfaction with how their lives have played out surface elsewhere as well. The film begins by quoting the opening of Dante's *Inferno*: 'Midway in the journey of our life / I came to myself in a dark wood, / for the straight way was lost' (2000: 3). Guédiguian points to the passing of time: 'Mon premier film se passait en face d'une cimenterie en pleine activité, mon septième enregistrait sa démolition, mon onzième film montre la pinède qui a repris ses droits là où elle était implantée.'[6] These statements capture the sense that the characters' lives have progressed down a path that cuts them off from their desires for more open, if non-conformist and even utopian, relationships to others. Their narrative takes place at a slippage point where the communal living of the past has completely disappeared. The characters are all looking for something beyond their world (with everyone's 'petty problems' as Marie-Jo puts it). Hence Daniel has also quit his successful construction business to teach others how to build, but when his apprentices selfishly demand a raise, he quits that too. Given how deeply they are constrained by their bourgeois lifestyle, it is not surprising to see that all of the characters must suffer from Marie-Jo's relentless desire for both men.

What is surprising is that they make such a strong effort to accommodate the situation, to avoid moral judgement and to disavow a proprietary relationship over Marie-Jo. Marie-Jo's daughter is the strongest defender of a proprietary attitude towards marriage: she taunts her father with images of Marco in bed with Marie-Jo, 'his sex in the place of yours'. Daniel is tempted by this view: when he finds out about the affair he brusquely seizes her as she undresses in the bathroom, but then he releases her and offers his hand, which she accepts. Marco empathises with Marie-Jo's suffering and no longer accuses her of having a 'comfortable' situation; he agrees that they

> to her. In another shot, filmed in a Mediterranean sunrise, on the boat after Marie-Jo and Daniel have made love, the couple should be at its happiest, but a close-up of her face, with Daniel out of focus in the background, shows her crying in solitude.

6 'My first film took place facing a fully active cement works; my seventh recorded its demolition; my eleventh shows the brush reclaiming the space where it was erected.'

should continue to live apart as 'eternal fiancées'. Neither man wants to constrain her, nor even hurt the other man: when Marie-Jo goes so far as to introduce them there is even a spark of sympathy between the two. They are indeed two 'amours' and not two 'amants'. For her part, Marie-Jo wants to be with both men, tells each of them that she loves him and the other, and, as she puts it, 'is only happy when she is making love'. All of these characters, and especially Daniel and Marie-Jo, are attempting, against family and social norms, to live their lives according to other systems of value.

The characters never do give up searching for this other way of living, but their experiment ends in tragedy. The penultimate scene is reminiscent of Jean Vigo's underwater superimpositions uniting separated lovers in *L'Atalante*. In this film we have two boats, Marco's ship and the little domestic pleasure craft that Daniel has given to Marie-Jo. Daniel and Marie-Jo leave port one morning, in a light that gives the utopian hue to the entire film. But in setting the anchor, Daniel slips and bumps his head: the fall has no causal tie to Marie-Jo's affair but is a accident of pure contingency; it is not a 'consequence' of her affair. When he falls overboard, Marie-Jo leaps in after him, and dives so deep that she cannot resurface. We watch the couple floating underwater, Marie-Jo's hand lovingly grasping his, but we also see superimpositions of Marco on his boat. Unlike the lovers in *L'Atalante*, who eventually come together in the flesh, the three here come together as a community possible only in death. The last shot returns to a society that seems cold and institutional: the more bourgeois Julie and Sylvain pick up her parents' belongings at the morgue when her mother's telephone rings, a kind of call from beyond that turns out to be from Marco. Marco and Julie represent one more missed connection, for there had been a genuine sympathy between them until Julie learned of the affair. Here she can only tell him through tears that 'Ce n'est plus la peine d'appeler, ils sont morts.'[7] Their experiment in living a utopian life has ended, and the world is slightly less cohesive, slightly worse off in their absence.

---

7 'It's no use calling; they are dead.'

Mon père est ingénieur (2004)

In *Mon père est ingénieur*, Guédiguian returns to a more familiar post-communist, Marxist heterotopia, seeking out what Fredric Jameson, in a text on Ernst Bloch, has called 'an imaginary enclave within real social space', an expression that could describe much of Guédiguian's practice (Jameson 2005: 15). The narrative is familiar: it includes a juxtaposition of local and global politics, an enlarged family, and a thematic concern for memory. Natacha (Ascaride) and Jérémie (Darroussin), both doctors, once formed a young, politically idealistic couple, but now they are living separate lives. Natacha, who had wanted to remain at home in Marseilles to live in a housing project and provide health care to its inhabitants, has inexplicably fallen into a mental torpor: she cannot speak or react and only moves when helped along by someone else. Jérémie has a more prestigious job, working in the health ministry in international health. Passing through Marseilles, he hears of Natacha's illness and decides to do what he can to help, staying in her apartment in the meantime. The profession of the two characters embeds the narrative somewhat ambiguously in a world health-care system that, though it retains universal coverage in France, contains many shortcomings, especially globally, due to economic conditions. Jérémie deals, unsuccessfully, with the frustration of providing health care on an international scale, complaining about how drug companies overcharge for AIDS medicine, leading to a situation in which his hands are permanently tied by geopolitical powers. Spending time in Natacha's apartment complex gives him a renewed sense of local usefulness as he helps a young girl with her homework and an immigrant man whose child is sick.

Though Natacha's local activism seems more promising, it is here that the trauma has struck. Working with Vadino (Meylan), in a housing project that Hamzaoui describes as 'a habitat shaken by urbanism', Natacha has successfully organised resistance to the eviction of some families. The two leaders pepper their speeches with the solidarity rhetoric of local activism and even sleep together (despite Vadino's wife) after their campaign. But Vadino, in his personal life, falls into a self-protective stance: when his fourteen-year-old daughter Mylène starts to spend too much time with an Arab boy he does everything he can to separate them. This is another echo of the Romeo and Juliet theme from *L'Argent fait le bonheur* and *À la place du cœur*.[8] Vadino's racism has roots in the fear of precarity: as an underemployed dishwasher, he wants a better life for Mylène, which will be difficult to attain if she marries an Arab. Later, Natacha must protect the girl when Vadino finds her and beats her, but he and his wife resent Natacha's meddling and finally her former comrade confronts her in her apartment and violently rapes her – the trauma that has caused her catatonic stupor. In this way, the film throws the political commitment of each character into doubt, Jérémie's at global level and Natacha's at local level.

The film's action is frozen at a present moment in which Jérémie and her family can only look on, but it shifts to a more diverse temporal experience inside Natacha's mind. It opens with a voiceover reading a comic-book adaptation of a story about the 'santons', the small clay nativity figures made in the south of France, among which one finds biblical figures alongside characters from other traditions such as the donkey and the cow and various human types from the 'village' of Bethlehem. The voiceover reading of the story by Natacha's mother (Pascale Roberts) is accompanied on screen by images of Ascaride and Darroussin playing Mary and Joseph, arriving in a kind of industrial hangar and welcomed by Donkey and Cow (Banderet and Patrick Bonnel). We also see the santon story of Roustido, also played by Meylan, the richest man in Bethlehem, who similarly attempts to prevent his daughter's love marriage to a poor boy.

These scenes, buried deep in Natacha's subconscious mind and unleashed by the trauma, allow the film to reconceive an image of utopia. Compared to the principal narrative, these scenes are shot differently (again by Berta), somewhat like *Marie-Jo et ses deux amours*, in softer light and colours, with many off-whites and blues. The borders disappear between fiction, religion, communism, folklore and reality, between real space and the abstract space of her mind. (The manger itself is in an abandoned warehouse or hangar.) Her turn to this enclave seems necessary for her to tap into the hope of these stories of her childhood (brought back by her mother), the hope of religion itself and to see, through these palimpsests, the analogies between vastly different periods. This is one of Guédiguian's most Blochian films, probing the impulse towards a better life in a hermeneutics

8 For a full treatment of this theme, see Kantcheff 2013: 178–81.

aimed at both everyday experiences and the stories and myths we tell. The religious texts are thus secularised, just as the everyday is, as Guédiguian puts it, 're-enchanted'.

During the long stretches of time waiting for Natacha's state to change, Jérémie takes stock of their past life together, again through flashback. The couple had met in a Russian class they were taking together as young communists: 'My father is an engineer' was the kind of high modernist utopian communist phrase that not only gave Jérémie difficulties in pronunciation but also reflected his ambition to make a global-scale impact, bringing him away from Natacha. Working in Natacha's space he disengages from his ambitious life, and he will probably leave his wife and move back: the film redirects us to local activism. Natacha is a more difficult problem. Though they throw drugs and shock treatment at her, nothing seems to wake her from her sleep. In the end, Jérémie decides to bring her back home to her apartment, the space of her work. As he carries her across the threshold he asks, 'On continue?' (Shall we continue?) The film ends with a teasing happy ending by cutting to black but including, only on the soundtrack, her response: 'On continue.' All she needed was another to provide her with strength.

Mon père est ingénieur reconnects the future to utopian folds and fragments of the past, to the imagination and to moments of love, friendship and resistance. Once again, an image of Darroussin and Ascaride from earlier work, a photograph of them kissing, probably a still or a set photo from *Ki lo sa?*, reconnects the past and future. What is not clear is the exact content of the future, but continuity itself implies that the future grows out of relation, even while remaining, at least here, in a virtual, Blochian, 'not-yet-conscious'.[9] Guédiguian thus also shares the same position that Bloch shares 'with existential philosophers, perhaps more with Sartre, for whom the future is praxis and project' (Jameson 2005: 7). At the same time, by once again directing the viewer outside of the film towards his own praxis, Guédiguian suggests that the future can be constructed through friendship, of which this cinematic project is an important example.

---

9 See the above discussion of this notion in the section on the happy ending in *L'Argent fait le bonheur*.

National identity: solitude, communism, friendship as resistance

Le Promeneur du Champ de Mars (2005)

Guédiguian's next film could hardly be set in a more distant political territory from proximity politics. In part, this is because *Le Promeneur du Champ de Mars* was a commission. In 2003, old friend Frank Le Wita came to Guédiguian with the project of adapting Georges-Marc Benamou's book, *Le Dernier Mitterrand* (Le Wita had hoped to make a television series of it, but Mitterrand's family objected, and a cinematic adaptation gave more freedom; Danel 2008: 108). Mitterrand, who had taken a liking to Benamou, had given him intermittent access over the course of several years in order to write a chronicle of his latter times in office (and thus some of the last days of his life, since Mitterrand famously hid from the public the fact that he was in a later phase of terminal cancer at the time). Working with Gilles Taurand, Benamou wrote the screenplay, though Guédiguian has said that he himself added a 'commie layer' (*une couche coco*) (Danel 2008: 108). It is the first film signed by Guédiguian for which he did not receive co-writing credit, which does not include any of his core actors and which does not take place anywhere in the vicinity of L'Estaque.

The project raises the question of Mitterrand's legacy. Biographies of Mitterrand (1916–96) range in judgement from hagiography to character assassination. The most substantive English-language biography, Ronald Tiersky's *François Mitterrand: The Last French President*, emphasises Mitterrand's victory over the Communist Party, his role in legitimising the presidency of the Fifth Republic and his support for European political and monetary unity at a time when a polarised Yalta–Europe was reorganising. Tiersky's Mitterrand had a Machiavellian political genius combined with a republican vision of the future that allowed him eventually to exert a broad influence over history. Tierksy underscores Mitterrand's charisma and his seductiveness, and especially his attachment to an existentialist freedom from the world he was acting upon. Accordingly, Tiersky claims that Mitterrand was exceptional, a reflection of the French exception itself, both in France's connection to republican ideas and in its ability to wield influence. Tiersky's subtitle echoes an often-quoted sentence from Mitterrand himself, one that originates in Benamou's book: 'Je suis le dernier des grands présidents. Après moi il n'y aura que des financiers et des comptables.'[10] Mitterrand is identified with an older, exceptional France (where the president could, without major scandal, have two families), epitomised in its great history and literature that Mitterrand knew so well, but a France now being integrated into a shifting world of Europe and globalisation.

Benamou's book provides a chronicle of Mitterrand's last period, his ill health and his departure from the Elysée Palace. It is hagiographic and soap-operatic at once, fascinated not only with Mitterrand as a charismatic and imperious figure but also with gossip, political rivalries, the president's mistresses, his gourmandise. (The rumour of Mitterrand's favourite meal of ortolans – tiny buntings caught alive, gorge-fed and literally drowned in Armagnac, an illegal dish nowadays – originated with this book.) The film sidesteps most of the tell-all sensationalism, in part by avoiding the slightest mention of Mitterrand's or his cronies' names; it is wholly focused on the president as a figure of French power.

This explains the choice of Michel Bouquet to play the leading role: in his long cinematic and theatrical career, Bouquet's charm and aristocratic air, along with imperious and enigmatic qualities, have made him a perfect fit for roles of kings and aristocrats. The film retains the premise of a young journalist, Antoine (played by Jalil Lespert), summoned by the president to follow him during his daily business and interview him to prepare the book. Antoine 'poses the same questions as [Guédiguian]': questions about Mitterrand's political positions and abandonment of the leftist cause, his Vichy past and his political opportunism (Audé and Tobin 2005: 28).[11] But Bouquet's Mitterrand dominates the film. In his review, François Bégaudeau perceptively notes the 'mute inserts' of the president's interlocutors, including Antoine, as they give him birthday gifts: he comments on each, which they have chosen with care, and dismissively tosses them to the side. Mitterrand fills the screen so much that other scenes – the story of Antoine's marital problems, the birth of his child and his eventual meeting with a new woman – are relegated to afterthought

---

10 'I am the last of the great presidents. After me there will only be financers and accountants.'
11 Antoine is decidedly more critical and left-wing than Benamou, who later became a close adviser to Nicolas Sarkozy before a rupture.

status. The editing is also political: the film cuts from Bouquet's pronouncements to Antoine's discussions with Mitterrand's former Resistance partners concerning when the president joined them, only to have his research dismissed by the president with a brush of a hand. The Mitterrand of the film is a portrait of a dying president who is also the monarch of France.

Herein lies an ambiguity that is also the problematic, or, according to some, the problem, of the film. This representation of a president-king is particularly hard to swallow for Bégaudeau, who wrote an intelligent negative review for *Cahiers du Cinéma*. Bégaudeau recognises the originality of Guédiguian's work in general, and its commitment to the *mise en scène* of 'la parole politique'. At the same time, the scenes in Chartres and Saint-Denis, discussing the kings in the royal necropolis of France, or quoting Péguy, suggest for him that Guédiguian is making an argument for Mitterrand as an embodiment of 'la France éternelle' (Bégaudeau 2005: 29). He finds the film overinvested in Mitterrand as a charismatic person, adored by and disdaining his cronies, an inspiration to the common man, even to an adolescent girl who stops him on the Champ de Mars to ask for a kiss. Bégaudeau is incensed to see Guédiguian tread lightly on Mitterrand's Vichy past and his questionable defence of workers in France.

Ludovic Cortade echoes Bégaudeau's criticisms of the film and gives them a deeper scholarly articulation, especially in Guédiguian's treatment of landscape. Indeed, the president's whims take him on helicopter detours over the plains of the Beauce, side trips to Chartres, a train to Brittany and visits to the chapel in Jarnac or the mausoleum of the Basilica of Saint-Denis to lay his hands on the tomb of François I. For Cortade, there is an identification of the aristocratic Mitterrand with the French landscape, one that furthermore takes place panoptically, from above, as if he were simply overseeing his national possession. For Cortade, the film seems to regret, at the death of Mitterrand, a lost unity between leader and people, a regret that forecloses on any future politics. *Le Promeneur du Champs de Mars* would be a kind of heritage film of the recent past, nostalgic for the *corpus mysticum* of the president-king.

But these criticisms may be too vigorous, for the film seems rather undecided on Mitterrand. As Bégaudeau laments, 'Guédiguian neglects to give a clear status to the generous verbosity of the President' (2005: 27). Bégaudeau's review begins with the observation that when Guédiguian leaves Marseilles, his films become all grey: not the many-nuanced grey that, according to the president, is the 'colour of France' (the 'purplish grey of lilacs and lavender' or the 'greenish grey of champagne') but 'grey of dullness'. The film, shot again by Renato Berta, bleeds the colour from the image; if this is Eternal France, then it is listless and abstract, as is especially noticeable at a beach scene in Brittany when the president pulls Antoine to one side and they walk in their dark clothes against the white sand and grey sky, nearly abstract shapes in an empty space. The president has access to every part of France, but wherever he goes, he's alone – flying over Chartres in his helicopter, in the underground mausoleum of Saint-Denis, or lying on the floor of the chapel in Jarnac. Moreover, in these solitary scenes, such as in the mausoleum running his hands along the marble of François I's tomb, he is in the dark and separated from the viewer by multiple frames, made up in this case of other tombs and pillars. Other scenes emphasise Mitterrand's weakness of body, especially in a shot of him unable to climb out of the bathtub without Antoine's help. The monarchical image of France is dying, and the president is a solitary, tragic figure: he may have an admirable imperiousness, but the representation of Mitterrand is far too ambiguous to inspire much nostalgia.

This ambiguous representation returns the one time that the film takes literally the '*mise en scène* of a political discourse'. In the book, Benamou describes a socialist meeting in Liévin that took place in 1994 and in which a new party secretary was to be appointed, resulting in in-party bickering. He cynically refers to the congress as 'doing *Germinal*' *(faire Germinal)*, since Liévin was also the setting for parts of Émile Zola's *Germinal*, one of the canonical texts of the labour movement in France; it was also the scene of a mining accident that claimed several lives in 1974. Guédiguian, who added the scene to the screenplay, gives the congress a more serious tone: there are a few cronies, but there are mainly workers gathered in the courtyard. Standing at a makeshift podium, the president's voice gathers strength as he reiterates the need for the left to defend workers: 'A victory on the left is possible under one condition: that we never forget that our family is the workers, the wage earners, the people who struggle.'[12] The camera cuts back and forth between the president and the workers gathered (faces 'blackened by modernity', as Bégaudeau puts it), who listen, their eyes raised, but the camera at their level: his words seem to connect deeply. At the end of the scene, however, we see one of the president's men snapping photos of the crowd. Was the old man inspired by a real connection (and a critique of contemporary socialists) or merely able to muster one more publicity stunt, pure *mise en scène* of a president who manipulates the people?

This indeterminacy is at the heart of Antoine's anxiety towards the president. Later in the film, sad and alone on his apartment balcony, a few disconnected images of Liévin come back to him: one of the workers from the earlier scene; a tentative approach to the courtyard filmed from a slow-moving car, in the rain; a few views of the village; all without any sound or other human presence except the voiceover of Bouquet's voice reading a speech. He argues for public ownership of industries, denounces monopolies and finishes with a diatribe against money: 'money that corrupts, money that purchases, money that crushes, money that kills, money that ruins, money that rots down to the very conscience of men.' This phrase did not come from the Liévin speech but from an address that a younger and more militant Mitterrand gave in 1971 at the Congress of Epinay, where he led a coalition of left-wing groups into the Socialist Party and won the party leadership: it was the beginning of the ascendency of the French left nationally, the beginning of Mitterrand's rise towards the top of French power, but also the beginning of the fall of French communism. But Antoine cannot reconcile these more militant words with the old man he has been observing.

At the film's end, Antoine helps the president from his bed into a chair so that he may look out a window at an old tree. The president speaks of biographies and the 'final words' of important people, which he finds unsatisfying. So he cuts the speech short with 'C'est fini' (It's over), and many unanswered questions. Cortade gives an impressive reading to the possible national signifiers evoked by the tree, ranging from the political (likening it to Mitterrand's 'tranquil

---

12 'Une victoire à gauche, n'est possible qu'à une seule condition. Ne jamais oublier que notre famille, ce sont les ouvriers, les salariés, les gens qui peinent.'

strength' campaign), to the nationalist (picking up themes of 'enracinement' from writers like Barrès), to the republican (such as Hugo's poem on 'liberty trees'), once again 'unifying' the president-king with the landscape (Cortade 2009: 76–8). But *mise en scène* again creates only distance: we see the tree through a grilled window, from a dark room and from behind the dying president. Antoine is reduced to standing by until the president dismisses him so that he can die alone. This is pretty cold nostalgia, but Cortade is right to assess the film as 'acknowledgement of powerlessness' rather than a 'critique of national identity' (2009: 78). The film presents a nation devoid, to quote Bégaudeau, of something 'bassement matérielle qui s'appelle la politique' (something basely material, known as politics) (2005: 29).

Voyage en Arménie (2006)

If Guédiguian uses *Le Promeneur du Champ de Mars* to explore political identity at a national level, *Voyage en Arménie* examines identification with origins, this time his own. The Armenian nation has corresponded to an autonomous, independent state only briefly. Balloted between the Persian, the Ottoman and the Soviet empires, Armenian culture had always been strongest in provinces in today's eastern Turkey, near Mount Ararat. Constant oppression culminated in the 1915–16 genocide at the hands of the Young Turks. Razmik Panossian has explained that during the genocide, the 'central point (the provinces) of Armenian identity was eliminated' and that most of those who weren't killed were left to survive 'in the form of diasporacized refugees concentrated in the Middle East, with some in France, Greece and elsewhere' (2006: 232). In many ways, feelings of Armenian belonging are strongest in the post-genocide diaspora. Many of these refugees settled in Marseilles, where Guédiguian's grandfather, who had arrived in Marseilles not long before the genocide to study theology, became actively involved in helping them. All of this aside, and despite these origins, Guédiguian came slowly and reluctantly to making a film about Armenia (see Mai 2015). His attitude towards his national origins, both Armenian and German, has always been relative indifference, unlike his firm attachment to questions of economic class and local place, in ways that echo proletarian internationalism: in an interview after the film's release, Guédiguian refers to himself as an 'classic old Marxist'.[13]

This return to identity comes in a conflicted French context at a moment when France was experiencing civil unrest in its cities' suburbs, when the Interior Minister, Sarkozy, made his infamous 'racaille' (scum) comment about the rioters and not long before the so-called 'debate on national identity' was launched by President Sarkozy. In 2010, Sarkozy made his own voyage to Armenia (where he remains popular) and called for Turkey to recognise the genocide. The following year, he lobbied the National Assembly to adopt a law making it illegal to deny all genocides, including the Armenian one. At the same time, France was opposed to the inclusion of Turkey in the European Union. What makes Guédiguian's return to Armenia, and national identity generally, different from Sarkozy's political appropriation?

Alain Badiou's writings on Sarkozy may clarify the question. Like Guédiguian, Badiou writes in search of a productive reference point outside of party politics, indeed outside of all electoral politics. He proposes an ideal, the 'communist hypothesis', which he hopes can orient political opposition against prevailing economic and cultural trends. In an echo of Guédiguian, Badiou catches glimpses of the communist hypothesis in local movements in which unaffiliated political actors reject the figures of 'passive and stereotyped consuming individuals' (Badiou 2008: 39). These rallying points are located, Badiou argues 'outside of the police' and can be found if the search is driven by what he calls an overarching 'performative' conviction: the unifying idea that 'there is only one world' (Badiou 2008). On a global level, the sentiment that there is only one world resonates nicely with the end of Yalta–Europe: the fall of the Wall in Berlin opens up the global horizon of a single world. But, for Badiou, economics and the police have betrayed the promise and erected new walls. Globalisation has facilitated the dominance of neo-liberalism, engendered more inequality and exclusion and

13 'For a very long time I took very little interest in these questions of belonging. I was born in a neighbourhood of Marseilles that was very structured, and I've always divided the world between rich and poor, and not between German, Italian, Armenian, Arab or Spanish. I continue to think, more or less, like a classic old Marxist, that this is the only conflict that really merits interest' (cited in Goudet, undated, unpaginated).

deprived workers of 'the basic right to move around and settle where they wish' (Badiou 2008: 55). The developing world is locked out of an economic progress that feeds the bank accounts of a rich minority.

Badiou's 'single world' contradicts precisely this type of barrier-building without denying the reality of self-identification with a national heritage. Badiou distinguishes between a world of sameness – a world 'closed in on itself' and 'different from another world' – and his ideal of a single world 'where an unlimited set of differences exists' (Badiou 2008: 63). In a single world, 'the transcendental measure of identificatory intensities, and thus of differences, is accessible everywhere to all, inasmuch as it is always the same' (Badiou 2008: 62). From this non-exclusive point of view, in a single world, everyone has a right to her own investment in sources of identity. What is not envisioned – and here is the important qualification – is for difference to be exploited by a police state to drive wedges between groups of sameness. According to Badiou, politicians and complicit intellectuals exacerbate differences and 'national identity' through figures of division. Sarkozy's positions are designed to distract the 'consumer': he uses Armenia to create a division with Turkey.

Le Voyage en Arménie is a road movie about a doctor of Armenian origins, Anna (Ascaride), who 'returns' to a country she has never known at a time when the ideal of 'one world' and globalisation are in serious conflict. Her return begins when Anna's father, whom Anna has diagnosed with cancer, leaves for Armenia, in part, he says, to 'teach her a lesson'. Anna has no interest in her origins: she doesn't watch her daughter dance, and even the old men playing backgammon in the Armenian cultural centre – her father's friends – do not recognise her. But, to settle matters with her father, she leaves: a coerced road movie resembling Guédiguian's own return.

What takes place once she arrives is basically a Guédiguian film like many others: not a film about a closed group identity but a film about friendship. It is organised around a series of encounters with people that Anna will need in her quest to find her father in Yerevan. At first she is grateful to meet Sarkis (Simon Abkarian), who travels to and from Armenia on business. But Sarkis is a slick-haired and ruthless businessman through whom Guédiguian introduces the viewer to a post-Soviet Armenian economy. En route from airport to hotel, from inside his luxury SUV (and over the techno music blasted by his driver), Sarkis explains a ferociously neo-liberal version of the new Armenia and offers his views of Armenians: communism has made them lazy and envious, but there are myriad new opportunities for doing 'business'. As they drive through nondescript gas stations (and a few flower shops), hinting at a global conformism, Anna is forced to confront some of her own contradictions: when she argues in favour of communism, he jokes that he would be a communist too, if he could afford it (the viewer is reminded of her swanky Mercedes).

But during the search for her father – the film exploits the temporal drift and openness of the road movie genre (see Gott 2013: 79) – Anna makes a number of deeper encounters that quickly turn into friendships. The first is with Schaké: a young hairdresser eager to make her way to the West and who resorts to topless dancing and working on the black market to make a living for herself, her grandmother and her sister. Her parents died during an earthquake, and the three women share a two-room shanty on the edge of town that she shows to Anna. Unlike for Sarkis, who has money, the borders remain daunting for poor people like Schaké. Another new friend, Simon, is a French doctor who operates a free mobile clinic in Yerevan. Though a less central character, Simon represents an alternative attitude towards the medical calling: if Anna's professional life has produced social status, a professional disposition and a nice car, Simon has dedicated himself to the poor at the clinic.[14] Yervanth is a Marseillais ex-pat of Armenian origins who was a member of the ASALA (Armenian Secret Army for the Liberation of Armenia) terrorist group in the late 1970s. In exile for his participation in an armed bank robbery in France, he arrived during the territorial war over Karabagh (given to Azerbaijan by the Soviets). He is still called 'The General', but he presently works in Yerevan as a kind of potentate in the same 'business' as Sarkis. His approach, however, is in opposition to that of Sarkis: it is Yervanth, for example, who buys medicine and funds the dispensary operated by Simon. Anna learns

14 Through Simon, Guédiguian addresses the issue of health care in Armenia and other developing economies, echoing another point of Badiou's 'communist hypothesis', the conviction that every sick individual should have a right to 'the present conditions of medicine' (Badiou 2008: 49). Armenia, the film suggests, is failing terribly in this regard, for there is no social-security system, no state insurance and little affordable medicine. This film about Armenian identity is highly critical of the status quo in Armenia itself.

a great deal about Armenia's sites of memory, international capitalism and herself through discussion and time spent with these new friends. It is through these dynamic relationships in the present that Anna comes to self-identify as Armenian herself rather than through her past. When she catches up to her father, she introduces to him her new Armenian 'family'.

Anna's friendships strongly reinforce her convictions and have a positive impact on her actions as can be seen in the violent narrative event that returns the film to action. All the narrative lines are connected in an über-capitalist health-care plot: Sarkis's illegal medicine trade is threatened by Schaké, who (with Sarkis's chauffeur) has been stealing it from the hospital and selling it on the side; Sarkis orders her murder; Anna saves the girl while shooting out the knees of Sarkis's henchman; Yervanth (founder of the dispensary) helps them escape to the countryside and finally settles accounts with Sarkis while issuing a stern warning: medicine will be allocated as it has been, perhaps not in the most legitimate and official way but to any and all and not according to profit. This is an imagined (if again implausible) micro-movement straight from the communist hypothesis: one world wins out, for now.

This story develops over images of landscape in which one can detect another commentary on national identity. For Armenians, the single most powerful natural symbol of Armenia is Mount Ararat, the site of the Haik and Bel story, in which Noah's descendant Haik rebels against Bel's Babylon and returns to the mountain and founds the country. The mountain is a symbol of 'righteous rebellion' and 'justice', evoked by nationalist movements (Panossian 2006: 51). Since Ararat is still located in Turkey, visible from Yerevan, the mountain continues to embody a painful loss. But Guédiguian avoids representing Ararat as a divisive national symbol. In fact, most images of the mountain in the earlier portions of the film are the tacky, touristic painting in Anna's hotel. Instead, Guédiguian shoots a diverse range of landscapes and architectures: traditional monuments such as churches, villages where women make bread in the old style and flower shops, but also gas stations, construction sites, a church that the Soviets did not destroy because it was too beautiful, a CNN building and, especially, the lower-class neighbourhoods and rubble on the outskirts. These images of rubble actually grow into a founding counter-myth of Armenia told by Yervanth as he flies Anna in a helicopter over the rock formations of the South Caucasus – not Ararat, but smaller fragments of the same formations. He tells her a story of their creation that displaces the myths of Noah, Haik and Bel. On the second day, God, here called a 'worker', passes the earth through a sieve to ensure that it is arable. (This good earth is in part what the 'have' countries have inherited – 'like France' Yervanth insists.) Like any good worker, God empties his sieve after his labours. He had forgotten, however, the barren rocks left inside, and which all fell to the ground in the same spot: Armenia. To belong to Armenia, the story suggests, means to be connected to its dregs: to the barren land, the earthquake-scarred hills that swallowed Schaké's parents and to Armenia's impoverished workers (with a continuity to wealthier countries such as France). From the helicopter, the camera sweeps across the barren rocks, the mountains bleeding out of the frame, with some craggy details in close-up, all over a music that combines traditional-sounding melody with modern instrumentation. This open and overflowing frame corresponds to a multiplicity of ways of identifying with the land.

Ararat only makes its way to the centre of the frame in an epilogue, a minor scene with important implications for Guédiguian's representation of national identity. Manuk, an aged chauffeur who has been driving Anna around Yerevan in Sarkis's absence, brings her to the airport to return to France. When he stops to retrieve a bumper that has fallen off his dilapidated car, he asks Anna to step out and look at the mountain. In Armenian, he tells her that a human being needs a dream and that his dream is Ararat. He brings up the Turks: 'One could imagine that the Turks are not like us, because of what they did.' But Manuk thinks that the Turks will return the mountain, not because of outside pressures or military force but 'because they know it is our dream' and 'they will feel better after they do'. In this way, Manuk lifts the film's message of friendship – among equals, the happiness of one gives pleasure to the other – to the level of national enemies. Being Armenian can, even must, take place in a single world. For Manuk, Ararat is a powerful symbol of economic worthlessness: even in Guédiguian's framing the real mountain appears to float like an unanchored abstraction, almost unreal, much like Manuk's dream of fulfilment and international friendship. But the cheap frames of the hotel paintings are replaced here, literally, with the real necks of construction cranes and electric wires that frame the mountain. To see the ideal that Ararat represents, we have to look beyond the new economic order that still stands to benefit from old divisions.

Le Voyage en Arménie does not avoid themes of national identification: on the contrary, to do so would mean conceding to the political class and the police state one more ideological tool for forging divisions. But Guédiguian's entry into the subject is proposing a more idealistic figure, according to which, as he states in a speech inaugurating the 'year of Armenia' in 2007, every person carries within 'the village where he is born' and 'the entire world' (Danel 2008: 121). Even Badiou uses the figure we have been pursuing throughout this project to describe the relation to the other at the international level: *friendship*, with the caveat that friendship should not remain a 'weakened form of traditional humanism' but become political – 'a friend is someone who exists in equality with yourself, in the same world as you' (Badiou 2008: 66). Or as Guédiguian used to tell his grandmother: 'Je préférais un Turc de gauche à un Arménien de droite' (Danel 2008: 19).[15]

L'Armée du crime (2009)

Guédiguian followed up Le Voyage en Arménie with another film about an Armenian on the left. Like *Le Promeneur du Champ de Mars* and *Le Voyage en Arménie*, the impetus behind *L'Armée du crime* came from somewhere else, in this case the film director Serge Le Perón. Le Perón had made a film about the assassination of Mehdi Ben Barka with the actor Simon Abkarian, and the two thought that Guédiguian would be a perfect fit to direct a historical film about the Manouchian group. As in *Le Promeneur du Champ de Mars*, Guédiguian concentrates on actors outside of his inner circle (most of the characters are younger than Guédiguian and his friends), though Meylan, Darroussin and Ascaride play secondary roles. For the communist and Armenian Guédiguian, Missak Manouchian was also a much more sympathetic and certainly less ambiguous figure than Mitterrand: if *Le Promeneur du Champ de Mars* drained the life out of Mitterrand's France, this film is a sincere effort in hero construction.

15 'I prefer a Turk on the left to an Armenian on the right.'

The Manouchian group was the Parisian division of the FTP-MOI (Francs Tireurs et Partisans/Main-d'Œuvre Immigrée), a Second World War resistance division of the Communist Party, made up mainly of foreigners. The Parisian cell was led by Missak Manouchian (Abkarian), an Armenian poet who had grown up in a Libyan orphanage after his family was killed during the genocide. In Paris, Manouchian led a group of Poles, Hungarians, Romanians and Italians, often of Jewish origin: many had already fought in Spain. During the occupation of France, they carried out sabotage missions and assassinations of German soldiers and officers. After an extensive investigation, and a betrayal under torture, the group was rounded up in November 1943, tortured by French police, handed over to the Germans for a mock trial and for the most part executed in Mont-Valérien in February 1944. Later that spring, the German authorities commissioned an infamous poster and flyer that were distributed to denounce the group. The 'affiche rouge' depicted, on a blood-red background, the faces of several members of the group, faces sullied and hair mussed, with captions that emphasised their foreign origins, their Judaism, or their adherence to communism. In large captions it read 'Des libérateurs? La libération par l'armée du crime!'.[16]

The Manouchian affair is one of the dark *faits divers* of the French occupation, but it has been memorialised in communist and leftist circles, most notably through a beautiful poem written by Louis Aragon, later set to music by Léo Ferré, based on Manouchian's last letter to his wife Mélinée. The episode has occupied a small place in the French high-school curriculum for some time. (Guédiguian, in an interview accompanying the American DVD of the film, says that his younger actors had vaguely heard of the group, though his film was now being played in schools across France.) The film has been praised as an effective (if hagiographic) entry into the Resistance film genre. Guédiguian concentrates on rewriting the image of those depicted on the poster and, in particular, Manouchian (the Armenian), Thomas Elek (a Jew born in Hungary) and Marcel Rayman (a Jew of Polish origin).

A few observers criticised the film for historical inaccuracies, most of which were entirely conscious on Guédiguian's part. A look

16 'Liberators? Liberation by the Army of Crime!'

at these reproaches gives a sense of Guédiguian's intentions and brings us right back to the wrangling over the legacy of communism, which we have analysed in Chapter 2. The most serious critique came, in an open letter published in *Le Monde*, from the historians Sylvain Bouloque and Stéphane Courtois, somewhat ironically since Courtois's book on the *groupe Manouchian* was one of Guédiguian's main sources. Bouloque and Courtois had a long list of reproaches. They criticised Guédiguian for presenting a group of unruly youngsters (whereas the FTO-MOI were a highly hierarchised group), for having one of them say he was not a Stalinist (whereas they were long-term party members), for suggesting that betrayal led to the arrests of November 1943 (they said it was due to competent police work) and, finally for emphasising the heroism of Manouchian (whom they saw as a reckless and naïve victim of communist manipulation). They attributed what they considered contempt for historical truth on Guédiguian's part to 'raisons idéologique et communautaire' (ideological and communitarian reasons) (Bouloque and Courtois 2009). We can translate 'ideological' to mean that Guédiguian's leftist tendencies supposedly make him neglect the role of the Soviets and paint the group as more independent-minded than they actually were. We can translate 'communitarian' to mean that the leftist Armenian, Guédiguian, inflated the importance of the leftist Armenian, Manouchian, at the expense of other partisans.

Guédiguian took the step of responding in a letter of his own to *Le Monde*, published a week later. In it he quoted Courtois's own book on the Manouchian group as evidence that the modifications he made were entirely conscious and plausible. But he pushed back hard against the accusation of ideological bias. First he referred to Courtois's now disproven hypothesis that the Communist Party might have purposely abandoned or delivered the group to the French authorities because they were foreigners and Jews. Courtois's hypothesis should be understood in the context of his other controversial historical work. His *Black Book of Communism*, for example, has been criticised for letting anti-communist ideology lead him to draw shaky parallels between Nazism and communists and paint all communist sympathisers as Stalinists.[17] Guédiguian admits freely that he creates

---

17 Courtois has also supported Gérard Chauvy, who has accused Raymond Aubrac of being a double agent working for Klaus Barbie.

from an ideological point of view, but he wants to make clear that his communitarianism is for what he calls, once again, 'la communauté des pauvres gens' (the community of poor people). He suggests that Courtois himself has ideological reasons for criticising the film in such loaded terms but that he is hiding those reasons behind his academic authority. The spectre of communism still seems to hover over this film.

The controversy (minor as it was) does give an idea of what Guédiguian was looking for in his 'legend'. He was trying to paint an image of the group as independent of strict communist control and trying to zero in on a small community forming among individuals in revolt. The film venerates not only the Armenian Manouchian but also two Jewish characters: the Hungarian Elek and the Pole Rayman. On at least three occasions, different characters – Elek's mother, another partisan from Hungary and Manouchian – mention leaving their homeland only to find a new 'family' in France. The characters all come together around this notion of familial bond and resist co-option from outside. Their ever-growing closeness helps them to survive and fight. It even helps them embark in difficult conversations, such as those through which they confront the moral issues of killing in resistance, which they agree is an obligation in this situation, though not to be performed indiscriminately.[18] Their bonds stretch across different ethnic groups: in one scene, Manouchian reminds the headstrong Elek, who had blamed his chief's inaction on the fact that he isn't Jewish, that Hitler, thinking of the Jews, had once famously declared, 'Who remembers the Armenians now?'

Despite the presence of historical figures, facts and even a shot of the Eiffel Tower, recognisable reference points are avoided in the film. Most of its spaces are intimate – kitchens, a family-owned shop or restaurant, or a park bench – accentuating the portrait of friendship rather than the historical circumstances. The casting favours youth and an androgynous beauty to contrast as fully as possible with the *affiche rouge*. These are young, clean (whence the several scenes of swimming and bathing), beautiful, refined and unaffiliated heroes

18 In one important scene they refuse to bomb a party because there are too many innocents (especially beautiful young women) in attendance. In another, Manouchian kills for the first time, but the image turns black and white, with a superimposed image of his brother, murdered during the genocide, contextualising the killing as a necessary political action.

of the working class, who, Guédiguian hopes, can provide a model for today: 'ce qui m'intéresse, c'est que cette histoire puisse éclairer la nôtre et fasse sens aujourd'hui' (Berthemin [undated]).[19] The film is thus diametrically opposed to *Le Promeneur du Champ de Mars*, the work it resembles the most, but where the ageing protagonist is alone, where there is no light (this work is filmed in colourful summer rather than grey winter), where space dominates humans and where no lesson for the future emerges. It is thus unsurprising that this thoughtful consideration of resistance and violence is now frequently used in French schools to tell the Manouchian story to a new generation.[20]

Masks and alienations

Lady Jane (2008)

Nestled between *Le Voyage en Arménie* and *L'Armée du crime*, two films dealing with history or collective identity, *Lady Jane* comes closer to Guédiguian's home turf and examines a more restricted social space. The film came to Guédiguian as he was filming Ariane Ascaride shooting a gun in *Arménie*, and from there grew into an edgy exercise in noir, in which he explores the genre's codes of violence. Muriel (Ascaride), who runs an upscale boutique in Aix-en-Provence, learns from a text message that her son Martin has been kidnapped and that she must quickly raise 200,000 euros to ransom him. She relocates two old friends in Marseilles, François (Darroussin) and René (Meylan), who help her raise the money. The terse first third of the film ends with an unexpected and brutal twist: Muriel arrives at a parking garage to make the exchange; her son walks towards her, wearing a smile; but then a shadowy figure runs quickly past and

---

19 'What I find interesting is how this story can shed light on our history and make sense today.'

20 Guédiguian's newest film, his nineteenth, *Une histoire de fou* (2015), also explores Franco-Armenian memory and moral issues surrounding acts of terrorism. The film was screened at Cannes in 2015, but unfortunately, and with a sad irony, released the week of the terrorist attacks in Paris on 13 November 2015. That weekend few people went to the cinema, and the film sold only 85,000 tickets before ending its run. As of this writing it has not yet been released on DVD.

shoots him in the back of the head: blood bursts out of the exit wound in his forehead as he falls slumped on the ground in front of his mother. The object was never to extort money, but to stage a murder. But who does it, and why, and how is Muriel to react to being the victim of such violence?

To answer these questions, the film sends us into fragmented flashbacks of the three friends' past. These start at the very beginning of the film, where we see them in the early 1970s donning rubber masks with the faces of grimacing old men with fuzzy grey hair, distributing stolen fur coats to the people of their neighbourhood. They wear the same disconcerting masks in a second flashback in another (or perhaps the same at an earlier time) parking garage. They have just robbed a jewellery broker in an expensive suit, Agostini, and are running away from the scene when Muriel stops to bait him: she shows him her arm, tattooed with a marijuana leaf and signed 'Lady Jane'. She knows that the man cowering before her has killed her father, himself almost certainly a mafia member (it was he who nicknamed her 'Lady Jane'). She points the gun at his head and pulls the trigger: another parking garage, another murder. Later, after trying to kill herself in despair at losing her son, Muriel replays the scene in her mind, as if the two events were linked, but without the thread that would tie them into a narrative.

In the terms of René Girard's theory of mimetic violence, Muriel's killing of Agostini marks her entry into the logic of vengeance, an 'interminable, infinitely repetitive process' (1977: 14). She has committed a single act, but by doing so she falls into the spiral of vendetta, a structural repetition of violence (the murder of her father calls for this killing) in which she now has no choice but to participate. She gains temporary satisfaction by killing Agostini, though the event seems to have disrupted her life: she is cleared by a argument of self-defence and moves away from Marseilles; she and her friends are separated, seemingly forever.[21] Returning to her friends now, she sets the cycle of bloodletting back in motion. The two men have remained, to different degrees, close to a criminal world: René is a strip-club manager, part-time pimp and small-time enforcer (he viciously beats up a barman); François, married with two children,

---

21 The setting of the film in Aix and in central Marseilles reflects the dissolution of community that one would usually find in L'Estaque.

has a legitimate boat-repair business but seems happy to slip back into crime. One night, François steals money and drugs from a group of dealers to pay the ransom. Later, when the dealers come back to threaten François, he murders all three of them, finishing one off with his bare hands. The killings proliferate.

Guédiguian effectively uses masks, retro clothing and other markers of film noir as physical manifestations of how the characters are deformed by violence. Even the anarchist theft of the coats at the beginning has something ominous about it, probably because the masks themselves are quite frightening and the overhead camera angle creates distance and disequilibrium. If the 1960s and 1970s should evoke hippies and folk music, this film opens with a dirtier, deeper, bass-driven blues. In the present, the characters wear external signs of edginess: baba-cool tattoos, Muriel's black raincoat and carefully styled hair and clothing. Many close-ups move in literally on faces, emphasising Ascaride's strict coiffure and austere clothes, Meylan's pockmarked cheeks and morose expression or Darroussin's walrus moustache. Once his drive towards violence is aroused, François gets carried away and begins to dress in the image of a gangster, trading his worker's sweater for a long fur coat, hat and pointed-toed shoes, the animal skins almost ritually marking his entry into violence. Other noir elements add to the ominous surface effects: dark lighting, numerous night scenes, muted dark red and browns, wintry outdoor shots, violence and suspense. Under masks, in the dark, the stream of violence flows more easily.

These signifiers of vengeance fall, however, at the climax of the film. The friends catch up to Martin's killer only to find out that he is in fact the twenty-something-year-old son of Agostini. They take him from his apartment and hide in an old schoolhouse, where Muriel admits to her friends, for the first time, that she had used them to kill Agostini. Agostini's son admits that he had been watching unbeknownst to them and saw her unique tattoo, which he again later spotted in a visit to Muriel's boutique with his wife. The spectacle of death at the beginning now finds its place in the narrative logic of mimetic violence: Martin was just one more unwitting victim in a larger spiral. The violence furthermore threatens to escalate again, since the young man (who has children himself) is kneeling on the floor with a gun to his head. It is at this point that something happens to lift the film out of the rising tide of vengeance.

For Girard, the bloody cycle of vengeance can only really be stopped, in a modern society, by 'the establishment of a judicial system – the most efficient of all curative procedures' (1977: 21). Indeed, only when 'an independent legal authority becomes *constraining*' are humans 'freed from the terrible obligations of vengeance' (Girard 1977: 21). Muriel refuses to speak to the police about her son's death, but the abandoned schoolroom where they take Martin's killer seems to perform the function of a court. In one of the rare daylight shots, the characters interrogate each other and confess what happened and why. But they also admit that their killing has not satisfied them. The scene is shot mainly in facial close-ups, showing the discomfiture of the actors' countenances – their masks – as they reveal their mixture of guilt and sorrow. Despite the long dialogue and explanations, which are perhaps too explicit, the scene is effective, mainly because each speech reveals the humanity of the speaker, their moral existence outside of the cycle of violence, to the others. Muriel is not constrained by some outside force when she prevents François from shooting Agostini; she does so out of understanding, of her guilt and his. The logic of vengeance has no more function: further killing would solve nothing since the other can no longer be a scapegoat. In the schoolhouse, each character seems to realise that the mask was alienation, a sign of their enslavement to the vendetta. The film too drops its mask of the film noir, showing itself to be a deeper exploration of violence and revenge.[22]

However, the unmasking takes place too late for a community to form: all the characters leave the schoolhouse alone. First, we see Agostini staring at his sleeping children, tears flowing down his face. Then François, unwilling to give up the disguise, literally puts on the mask from many years ago, breaks into a jewellery store and is shot in a kind of 'suicide by policeman'. René is a more distant character throughout: his motivations for the original robberies were political, to steal from the rich and give to the poor, and

---

22 There is an interesting comparison to be made with the crime novels of Guédiguian's friend, Jean-Claude Izzo, whose protagonist Fabio Montale is a police officer but one who is continually drawn from legitimacy into crime until his death: his sacrifice puts an end to the circle. Here Guédiguian's characters manage a way out through confrontation.

he has been sceptical of Muriel's act since the beginning. When François dies, in his arms, René simply gets out of the car, crosses the street and enters the nightclub: his life continues as before. In the film's final images, Muriel attends a techno concert, a ticket that her son had received in the mail after his death. She grips tightly the SIM card of her son's telephone (her last connection to him) and stands in his place, listening to his music, surrounded by dancing people his age and, in the blue and red light, cries and gently rocks her head back and forth. Perhaps, having dropped her mask, she is beginning to mourn, though it may also be too late. An old Armenian proverb that closes the film suggests the latter interpretation:

> Celui qui cherche à se venger
> Est comme la mouche
> Qui se cogne contre la vitre
> Sans voir que la porte est grande ouverte.[23]

Though Guédiguian explores vengeance in a microcosm, the film does suggest, subtly, that its themes of retribution and vengeance are relevant in geopolitics as well. In one scene, François, nostalgic for their old haunts, brings Muriel back to their neighbourhood in Marseilles to revisit the bar that was the centre of the neighbourhood life. Solange (Pascale Roberts), the wife of the owner, does not remember them or their silly fur coats, but her husband Henri (Boudet), though ill and confined to bed, has an all-encompassing memory. Vaguely resembling their old masks, Henri is sincere and has retained his righteous indignation from the earlier period. When they arrive, he is dozing in front of a documentary called *Les Années de sang: Israel – Palestine* (*The Bloody Years: Israel – Palestine*). The images and voiceovers in the background as they speak show victims, the powerful Israeli military, and also masked Palestinians with bazookas. 'Que des histoires de vengeance', exclaims Henri. (Nothing but stories of vengeance!)

---

23 He who seeks revenge / Is like the fly / Who beats its head against the pane / Without seeing that the door is wide open.'

Les Neiges du Kilimandjaro (2011)

If *Lady Jane* moves closer to L'Estaque, *Les Neiges du Kilimandjaro*, for the first time since *Marius et Jeannette*, is set there almost entirely. In various interviews, Guédiguian has called the work a 'film bilan'; through it, he re-evaluates his project, his group of friends and the type of characters they play, in their present situation, within the movement of power, labour and economic exploitation.

The film is thus filled with frequent evocations of past militancy, beginning with a rather retro-fitted first shot of a group of workers, solemnly gathered on the docks, where Michel (Darroussin) and Raoul (Meylan) read out, from scraps of paper chosen randomly from a hat, the names of twenty men who will be laid off from their jobs. Michel and Raoul, old friends, have overseen the lay-offs in the fairest manner possible: Michel, an old-school organiser, has even included his own name, chosen at number 19, though as the trade-union representative he was not expected to, and despite the fact that his age will make finding another job difficult. The scene paints him as a morally upright man, willing to sacrifice; he has a lifelong attraction to courage and heroes: Spiderman as a child and Jaurès from the time of his political consciousness. Acts of self-sacrifice such as this have brought Michel the accolades of friends and family. His co-workers pat him on the back, Raoul protests that he shouldn't have added his name, and his wife, Marie-Claire (Ascaride), laments, with indulgence, that it is 'hard to live with a hero'.

Kilimandjaro is in fact a film about moral righteousness, and this beginning is as preachy and exalted as anything Guédiguian has made. Michel lives an idealised life, even post-lay-off. Beyond holding everyone's esteem, he is the patriarch of his family, with children and grandchildren who adore him. He and Marie-Claire celebrate their thirtieth anniversary, where, surrounded by his friends and former co-workers at the party (he had invited all those who were laid off), Michel makes a speech about how much he loves his wife. Friends and family present the couple with a small treasure chest, which they open to find a stack of money and a small gift-wrapped package, filled with paper, which Michel jokingly guesses to be a copy of the Common Programme between the socialists and communists. It turns out to be his old Spiderman comic book (which Raoul had 'borrowed' many years ago) and in it a pair of tickets to a long-earned safari at the foot of Mount Kilimanjaro. This is Michel: a fusion of organiser, superhero and friend who merits a nice vacation. Everyone gathers around to sing an old song, led by the children, 'Les Neiges du Kilimandjaro'.[24] The mawkishness is thick, and eyes are misty; this is almost self-parody.

The fact is that Michel and Raoul, their wives Marie-Claire and Denise, though nice enough, begin to weigh on the viewers' nerves. The scene immediately following the party directly cites the famous card game from Pagnol's *Marius*: the four friends practically mug for the camera as they play cards, exchange neighbourhood gossip and accuse each other of cheating. This is far from the conversation in which friends draw out hidden qualities in each other. It may even come as welcome relief when two masked gunmen suddenly burst into the house, tie the four of them up with duct tape and take their money, bankcards and the plane tickets. While one gunman goes to verify the codes on the credit cards (one of them, problematically for someone who can afford credit, 1936, to honour the Front Populaire), the other pages through Michel's *Spiderman* comic, stealing it in the end. It is hard to feel sorry for him.

It is Michel who discovers the robbers when he bumps into a boy on a bus who is reading that rare copy of *Spiderman*: he follows him home and spots Christian, a young man laid off with him, who had even been to the anniversary party. The viewer, however, has seen Christian without his mask before Michel does. Guédiguian has already shown us that he is not just a thief nor even just a young worker looking for a job but the caregiver to his two brothers, whose too-young mother (the neighbour thought they were brother and

24 The eponymous song, originally released in 1966 and sung by Pascal Danel, tells the story of a voyager who finally arrives at the mountain after a long journey. He can rest, but the refrain implies that this is the end of his life: 'Elles te feront un blanc manteau / où tu pourras dormir / elles te feront un blanc manteau / où tu pourras dormir, dormir, dormir.' (The snows will make you a white mantle where you can sleep / they will make you a white mantle, where you can sleep, sleep, sleep.) The song echoes the hard journey of another pop song that fills the soundtrack in the early stages of the film, Joe Cocker's version of Jimmy Cliff's *Many Rivers to Cross*. But in Cliff's song we are beginning a journey with an uncertain future and must rely on pride and hard work to arrive. Though the songs share sentimental and thematic registers, they seem to be at opposite ends, one nearing satisfaction and one at the beginning of the quest. Together they seem to ask whether Michel is at the end or at the start of his life. Which way will he take?

sister) has left the family. Christian must prepare them for school and feed them alone, with a little help (to belabour the Joe Cocker references) from a cute neighbour. Robbing Michel was his first crime, and he could certainly fall deeper into criminality, but generally he seems like a decent person pushed to desperation, in part because of Michel's actions on the dock.

Guédiguian uses this film to recast Michel's initial political act, outwardly an act of selflessness, within a socio-economic situation in which it no longer seems to have the same weight, morally or politically. This is in part because History is again changing: the economic system and employment market have deteriorated to the point of creating a new underclass, what Guy Standing has called 'the precariat'. Standing argues that workers in the precariat are less and less prone and able to form collective-bargaining entities because the types of jobs that traditionally bring workers together disappear more and more; these workers experience low-skilled, short-term, flexible jobs, many of which require them to work alone and on their own time. It should be remembered, however, that there are divisions in this new class of labour. In the demographics of precarity, Standing describes two types of 'old-agers': the 'grinners' and the 'groaners'. Among old-agers, the 'grinners' are those with adequate pension and healthcare coverage, who can do odd jobs for the pleasure of activity or to earn money for extras; the 'groaners are those, without a reasonable pension, who face competition from more energetic youth and less needy old agers' (Standing 2011: 284). For Michel, a lifetime of hard work has brought him along far enough that he now owns a house and a retirement plan; he returns to work at a non-skilled job delivering publicity papers, mainly to supplement his pre-retirement. He is a grinner; or, as Steven Ungar puts it, despite being unemployed, he lives in 'the bubble of privilege' (2014: 285).

It is not easy to see the rest of the precariat class from inside this bubble and especially not the younger workers like Christian. Standing writes that in France, '75% of all young employees start with temporary contracts', and that fewer and fewer move on to permanent positions (Standing 2011: 65). A brief encounter between the two men in an employment office, before Michel realises Christian has robbed him, encapsulates their different places in the division of labour. Michel, who has arrived first, warns Christian that there are no welder jobs left, except foreign ones, but since Christian is young he has the flexibility to take one. To believe that Christian is more flexible is a very hasty conclusion based on prejudice towards the young, since Christian obviously cannot abandon his brothers. Furthermore, Christian's future is much bleaker than Michel's: Michel acts as if the stakes are the same for him as for Christian, except that Christian will have to deal with the shifting job market and shrinking social umbrella whereas Michel's future is assured by past labour victories. Christian is already turning to criminality. He is a groaner, and an unacknowledged one.

Much of the rest of the film consists of Michel gradually dropping his faulty perspective and learning to refocus on his moral place within the economic world. This is not easy: Christian's attack, beyond the material loss, has dislocated Michel's shoulder and given Denise, his sister-in-law and best friend's wife, a nervous breakdown. Raoul adopts a hard-line, Front National-type discourse on punishment, and Michel is so angry that he punches a handcuffed Christian in the face in a police interrogation room. Here it is Michel who seems to wear the false mask of the righteous union leader. The economic situation has successfully channelled everyone into practices of division: the criminal, the reactionary, the neurotic victim, in-groups and scapegoats.

If Michel is able to rise above pettiness, it is not because of his experience in the union or the party but because his communism has a moral dimension, one that reflects the definition of 'living together': i.e. he has the courage to step outside, to self-alienate and to judge his own place in history. He does this by considering a phrase from Jaurès that he had rather pretentiously cited in the past: 'Le courage, c'est de comprendre sa propre vie, de la préciser de l'approfondir, de l'établir, et de la coordonner cependant à la vie générale.'[25] He decides not to press charges. But this small act of generosity is not enough for the crime has been registered, and Christian will go to prison. Michel explains himself and apologises to Christian at the courthouse but instead of forgiveness Christian greets him with hostility and points out how the original drawing of names was unfair: another setback, especially since Christian is quite right and Michel could have looked at each man's situation to see who was

---

25 'Courage is understanding one's own life, to define and deepen it, to establish itself, and to coordinate it with life in general.'

most in need of a job. The landscape has shifted under his feet; every quality he had displayed in the beginning of the film is proven false. At the end of their interview, Christian ironically tells Michel that if he really wants to help he can stop by at his apartment to check the plants. It is there, of course, that he discovers what the viewer has been aware of all along: the boys, their uncertain future and the role of their brother in protecting them. He makes a decision that seems extravagant but that reflects his actual moral responsibility: to take them home to live with him until Christian is out of prison. Unbeknownst to him, Marie-Claire has come to the same realisation and has already been making dinner for the kids and watching TV with them in the evenings.[26]

Michel and Marie-Claire remake their married life by again redefining the family according to the need created by the new division of labour. Their children react negatively to the decision; successful in their professional lives, they have little perspective on the inequalities of the precariat. (The film gives them a remarkably negative treatment, like the daughter in *Marie-Jo et ses deux amours*.) Michel and Marie-Claire's action tests their friendship as well, but it turns out strong enough to change for the better: Raoul and Denise stop by the house at the end of the film and befriend the new kids. Says Raoul: 'Il parait que ça ne se fait pas. Mais entre nous, ça se fait.'[27] From Guédiguian's first film, trust between friends is strong enough to absorb the challenges and discords that make people grow.

The couple's spontaneous decision to take in the kids echoes a poem by Victor Hugo, titled 'Les Pauvres Gens', in which an impoverished fisherman and his wife independently resolve to take in the children of a dead widow, adding them to their own large family.[28] 'Les pauvres gens' is an expression that Guédiguian habitually cites in interviews and was the working title for this film before he opted

26 She also learns a lesson about judging from Christian's mother, whom she confronts with a certain superiority, only to learn that her problems are also serious and, in part, due to gender-specific economic difficulties.
27 'Apparently that's not something one does; but between us, you do.'
28 In the poem, the wife of a fisherman watches over her five children as she waits anxiously for her husband to return on a stormy night. Walking on the beach the next day she visits a sick widow, only to find her dead while her two children sleep. The fisherman comes home with little to show for his hard work, but he wants to take the children in and treat them as his own children. The mother pulls back the curtain on their bed, and there they are.

for the more ironic *Les Neiges du Kilimandjaro*. The simple phrase has the advantage of evoking a spontaneous solidarity while again avoiding affiliation with the institutions of a traditional left, institutions that can, as in Michel's case, produce hierarchy and cloud moral vision. Through this expression, Guédiguian reiterates the need for an effort to build solidarity where institutions have failed:

> Avant, la classe ouvrière était visible ... Et puis, il y avait ces autres espaces où les ouvriers se rencontraient: les syndicats, le parti communiste. Aujourd'hui, cette armée est disséminée, même si elle existe encore. Les nouveaux ouvriers portent des chemises blanches et travaillent au chaud, dans des bureaux: les employés de France Télécom, par exemple. Ils ne se considèrent pas comme des prolétaires, pensent disposer d'un statut supérieur, mais ils gagnent le smic. C'est terrible, cette absence de fédération des pauvres gens. Ils sont à la fois si nombreux et si seuls.[29]
>
> (Blottière 2011)

Au fil d'Ariane (2014)

Guédiguian and Ariane Ascaride explain the genesis of *Au fil d'Ariane* as a 'gift' that Guédiguian wanted to offer Ascaride after seventeen films together (Leclerc and Leherpeur 2014). Given its title, it is also a highly personal film, about 'following' Ariane, something Guédiguian has been doing, with a camera, for thirty-five years. It can be read as a film about acting and film-making, with love as the glue holding them together. It is also, through the ambiguity of the title, a gesture out of the narrative world, towards the practice of film-making together with friends, and, as such, it is a fitting film to begin a transition towards concluding this book.

Au fil d'Ariane, as Guédiguian adds, is a film about 'adventure'. The film is subtitled a 'fantaisie', and, as such, it deals somewhat less with

---

29 'Before, the working class was visible ... And also, there were places where workers could meet: unions and the Communist Party. Today, a working-class army is completely dispersed, even if it is still exists. New workers today wear white shirts and work in relative comfort, in offices: the employees of France Télécom, for example. They don't think of themselves as proletariat; in fact they give themselves a higher status, but they earn the minimum wage. It's terrible, this absence of a federation of poor people. They are, at once, so numerous and so alone.'

specific social issues. But, as 'fantaisie', it is presented as an escape from a certain type of social space. During the credit sequence, Guédiguian uses CGI graphics, white and blue, in the style of paper shapes much like an architectural model, showing a relatively chic apartment building. The camera travels through this colourless environment, where people have no faces or personality, where even the green of the interior park is artificial, until it reaches Ariane's apartment. It is her birthday, but she has to make her own cake, and, as she lights the candles, she receives voice messages from her two children and husband, who will not make it home. Despite Ariane's pink and white dress, this space is cold and insipid: adventure is welcome.

Soon after, Ariane is driving her Mini Cooper through an anonymous Marseilles. When a drawbridge holds up traffic, she meets a young man, and a series of encounters continues until the end of the film. The film has no real classical narrative but a very 'free' and dream-like succession of tableaux, bringing her into L'Estaque and surrounding areas, the space that Guédiguian has filmed since the 1980s. Discouraged by circumstances from going home (a stolen handbag, a taxi who refuses her fare), Ariane befriends a crusty café-owner, Denis (Meylan), a young woman who prefers to be a prostitute instead of a cashier (Lola Naymark), her boyfriend (Adrien Jolivet) and a Marseillais poet who pretends to be American (Boudet). She waits tables for the local retirees of the seaside café (the same restaurant as the Perroquet Bleu in *À la vie, à la mort!*), sleeps in a little boat in the port (though she also makes love to Denis), helps Raphaël and Lola with their relationship and befriends an elderly Cameroonian, Martial, who calls out at night to animals he has left behind in his country. The loose narrative gives Guédiguian the flexibility to insert scenes and shots that do not contribute to the narrative progression, often to surreal effect, as in the case of a turtle that talks to Ariane throughout the film. The rest of the film also contains post-production digital manipulation of colour, but here to emphasise the strong blues, purples and pinks of the settings and clothes.

Guédiguian calls *Au fil d'Ariane* a film 'without a head or a tail' but with 'a body', the body of Ariane Ascaride (Leclerc and Leherpeur 2014). But this body is not a fixed physical entity: 'being', for Ariane, as she explains in a humorous and messy wordplay on the verbs 'être' (to be) and 'suivre' (to follow), is wrapped up in following after, not only after her own self but also after others. To the degree that the narrative advances, it does so through movement towards those she meets, their own bodies and also their desires and problems. The most event-like actions of the film come when Ariane tries to help Martial, who is haunted in his sleep by animals that he has left behind, first in Cameroon, then at the zoo of Marseilles, and after that, when the zoo was transformed into a natural-history museum, the strange and bloodless animals kept in formaldehyde-filled jars. Ariane convinces the others to break into the museum and liberate these specimens, obvious metaphors for herself (and themselves), stuck as she is in a kind of aquarium, presenting no interest even to her family, with little possibility for change. As they drop the animals into the sea, a terrible storm, purposely filmed in grand adventure-film style, kicks up the waves: this impressive shipwreck leaves them lying on a sunny beach the next morning, on the Frioul Islands, a mere four kilometres from Marseilles. Encounter leads to adventure.

Perhaps the strangest turn, from a narrative point of view, is where this story ends up, at a theatre among Greek ruins on the island. Here we find an actor (played by Darroussin, who had also played Ariane's taxi driver), whose partner (and lover) is leaving him. (She's played by Anaïs Demoustier, who had also been a waitress at the café). The replacement of the same bodies in different roles and the difficulty of knowing whether this is theatre or reality compound the alienation effect. The film ends when Ariane herself, later that night, with a full audience in attendance, slips into the girl's cabaret costume and sings Brecht and Weill's 'As You Make Your Bed', to copious applause.[30] Guédiguian's *mise en scène* is filled with emotion: red and green colours, a flattering spotlight, even a screen split into nine images, showing Ascaride's performance from all angles. The scene draws intriguing connections between shipwreck, mythology, the theatre, friendship and adventure.

The scene provides an idea of what an implied viewer would be for a Guédiguian film. As Ascaride begins to sing, Guédiguian shows the arriving public, in a citation of Pasolini's *Gospel According to Matthew*,

30 We find out earlier that Ariane's mother was a singer and that she herself had always wanted to perform on stage, making this the realisation of a dream. There is perhaps a parallel here with Ascaride's father, a sales representative from L'Oreal and a hairstylist, who performed in amateur theatre and had wanted to be an actor.

as pilgrims descending the winding paths of the island.[31] They carry their dinner, in groups of friends, chatting on their way. They sit practically in the round, and the camera cuts from Ascaride's face to them and then pans across her friends as she sings. The setting evokes the *polis*, updated with Weill and Brecht's Marxist aesthetic. At the same time, the song is pure fun; everyone is entertained, relaxed and unhurried. The scene echoes a much earlier one in *Rouge midi* that takes place in a cinema house: the characters shake hands and chat in the lobby; two kids sneak in and shoot wads of paper through straws at older film-goers; one character bumps into an old friend back from college in Paris; people talk and react to the film. In both films, the cinema (or theatre) is, above all, a place of encounter, a space where we meet, are entertained and find matter for reflection, a thread leading us out of the labyrinth of our lives.

Ascaride plays an exceptional role in this encounter, at least as far as Guédiguian's cinema is concerned. One remarkable shot begins with a glowing, happy Ariane, dressed in bright red pants and a blue shirt, looking directly at the camera, smiling enigmatically (with a love song by Jean Ferrat playing on the soundtrack). The camera pulls back slowly, cranes up and turns towards the sea before turning straight up into an azure sky, where it waits for several seconds, though the sky itself turns golden, and the camera repeats its movement in the other direction, showing Ariane still waiting tables at night. The shot is a kind of loving portrait in homage to Guédiguian's partner but it also breaks momentarily the realist illusion in a way that interpolates the viewer directly. Ascaride is joyfully acknowledging the audience. The film's final shot brings us back to her home: the doorbell rings, and everyone is there; it was all a daydream. All of the actors gather around her, this time as members of her family or friends, even the turtle shows up. But there is something sad about this group, in this drably coloured world, the kids with their hipster glasses and Ariane almost crying as she kisses her husband. It is simply less interesting than the theatre or the seaside.

31 There are in fact multiple references to the history of cinema, including a completely gratuitous scene of the young characters playing and kissing in the fountain in front of the Marseilles Natural History Museum in a visual quote of Anita Ekberg and Marcello Mastroianni frolicking in the Trevi Fountain in Fellini's *La Dolce Vita*. Guédiguian calls them '*révérences*' rather than 'references', and they add to a style that combines moral warmth, myth and dream while reminding us that we are watching a film.

In each of these the three films I have grouped into this last section, characters wear masks: the mask of vengeance, the mask of self-satisfaction and, here, the mask of the bourgeois housewife, beneath which hides another mask, this one self-consciously worn: the mask of the actor. But this latter mask does not hide the person: rather, it functions for the person as a means to make new experiences. As Ariane Ascaride, the actress, puts it:

> Si j'étais restée dans le monde dont je suis issue, peut-être que nous ne pourrions pas nous parler. Et c'est cela qui me passionne. Toujours trouver les passerelles pour que moi, nous, qui parlons d'un monde qui n'est pas le vôtre, vous puissiez entendre. Et si vous entendez, si vous pouvez aimer les films de Robert c'est que, lorsque nous sommes ensemble, nous retrouvons nos pères et nos grands-pères et que nous sommes sincères.[32]

(Leclerc and Leherpeur 2014)

Acting means to participate in an ancient social rite. It means to drop the mask that one wears in the banal everyday world to pick up other masks, those that permit one to show oneself in a space of encounter with other people, other places, other experiences. *Au fil d'Ariane* thus reflects Guédiguian's practice as a whole, in which the division between the inside of the cinema and the outside of his personal life is blurred, as is obvious in so many of his films.

References

'*À la vie, à l'amour*: Interview avec Jean-Pierre Darroussin, Gérard Meylan, et Ariane Ascaride', *Télérama*, 26 June 2002, pp. 32–6.
Anderson, Philip (2008) 'Stories of Violence, Violence of History: The Political Logic of Guédiguian's Cinema from *Dernier été* (1980) to *La Ville est tranquille* (2001)', *The Australian Journal of French Studies*, 45:3, 238–49.
Audé, Françoise and Yann Tobin (2005) 'Entretien avec Robert Guédiguian: 'l'intérêt, c'était d'allégoriser Mitterrand', *Positif*, 528, 27–31.
Badiou, Alain (2008) *The Meaning of Sarkozy*, London: Verso.

---

[32] 'If I had stayed in the world from which I came, we would probably have nothing to say to each other. That's what impassions me about acting. It's always finding bridges so that I, or rather we who are talking about a world you do not possess, can make you understand anyway. And if you understand, if you love Robert's films, it is because, when we are together, we are back with our fathers and our grandfathers and we are sincere.'

Bégaudeau, François (2005) 'Le Promeneur du Champ de Mars', *Cahiers du cinéma*, 598 (February): 28–9.
Benamou, Georges-Marc (2011) *Le Dernier Mitterrand*, Paris: Plon.
Berthemin, Christophe (undated) 'Robert Guédiguian, réalisateur', *Frenetic Arts*, available at www.freneticarts.com/rcinema/interview.php?ID=40 (accessed 2 January 2016).
Blottière, Mathilde (2011) 'Robert Guédiguian: "C'est terrible cette absence de fédération de pauvres gens"', *Télérama*, 15 November, available at www.telerama.fr/cinema/robert-guediguian-c-est-terrible-cette-absence-de-federation-des-pauvres-gens,74900.php (accessed 2 January 2016).
Bouloque, Sylvain, and Stéphane Courtois (2009) '*L'Armée du crime* de Robert Guédiguian, ou la légende au mépris de l'histoire', *Le Monde*, 14 November, available at www.lemonde.fr/idees/article/2009/11/14/l-armee-du-crime-de-robert-guediguian-ou-la-legende-au-mepris-de-l-histoire_1267221_3232.html (accessed 2 January 2016).
Cortade, Ludovic (2009) 'The Spatial Evacuation of Politics: Landscape, Power and the "Monarch" in Robert Guédiguian's *The Last Mitterrand*', *Yale French Studies*, 115: 67–79.
Danel, Isabelle (2008) *Conversation avec Robert Guédiguian*, Paris: Les Carnets de l'Info.
Dante (2000) *The Inferno*, trans. Robert Hollander and Jean Hollander, New York: Random House.
Engels, Friedrich (2010) *The Origins of the Family, Private Property and the State*, ed. Tristam Hunt, London: Penguin.
Girard, René (1977) *Violence and the Sacred*, Baltimore, Md.: Johns Hopkins University Press.
Gott, Michael (2013) 'Traveling Beyond the National: Mobile Citizenship, Flexible Identities, and Layered Republicanism in the French Return Road Movie', *Contemporary French Civilization*, 38:1, 73–95.
Goudet, Stéphane (undated) 'Robert Guédiguian: "Par endroits, Erevan, c'est L'Estaque de mon adolescence ..."', *TV5monde*, available at www.universcine.com/articles/robert-guediguian-par-endroits-erevan-c-est-l-estaque-de-mon-adolescence (accessed 16 June 2013).
Guédiguian, Robert (2002) Note accompanying press release of *Marie-Jo et ses deux amours*.
—— (2009) '"L'Affiche rouge", cinéma, histoire et légende, par Robert Guédiguian (réalisateur)', *Le Monde*, 22 November, available at www.lemonde.fr/idees/article/2009/11/21/l-affiche-rouge-cinema-histoire-et-legende-par-robert-guediguian_1270203_3232.html (accessed 13 December 2015).
Izzo, Jean-Claude (2006) *La Trilogie Fabio Montale*, Paris: Gallimard.
Jameson, Fredric (2005) *Archaeologies of the Future: The Desire Called Utopia and Other Science Fictions*, London: Verso.
Kaganski, Serge (2001) 'Marseille: Ville ouverte', *Les Inrockuptibles*, 16 January, p. 39.
Kantcheff, Christophe (2013) *Robert Guédiguian, cinéaste*, Paris: Éditions du Chêne.

Leclerc, Fabrice and Xavier Leherpeur (2014) 'Ariane Ascaride and Robert Guédiguian: "*Au fil d'Ariane* n'a ni queue ni tête mais il a un corps"', *L'Express cinéma*, 16 June, available at www.lexpress.fr/culture/cinema/ariane-ascaride-robert-guediguian-au-fil-d-ariane-n-a-ni-queue-ni-tete-mais-il-a-un-corps_1551429.html (accessed 30 December 2015).

Mai, Joseph (2015) 'The Ideal of Ararat: Friendship, Politics, and National Origins in Robert Guédiguian's *Le Voyage en Arménie*', in Michael Gott and Todd Herzog (eds.), *East, West and Centre: Reframing Post-European Cinema since 1989*, Edinburgh: Edinburgh University Press, pp. 179–92.

Marx, Karl (1983) *The Portable Karl Marx*, New York: Penguin.

Morris, William (1993) *News from Nowhere and Other Writings*, London: Penguin.

Panossian, Razmik (2006) *The Armenians: From Kings and Priests to Merchants and Commissars*, New York: Columbia University Press.

Rascaroli, Laura (2006) 'The Place of the Heart: Scaling Spaces in Robert Guédiguian's Cinema', *Studies in French Cinema*, 6:2, 95–105.

Sotinel, Thomas (2001) 'Si Marseille, la vraie, m'était enfin contée', *Le Monde*, 17 January.

Standing, Guy (2011) *The Precariat*, London: Bloomsbury Academic.

Tierksy, Ronald (2000) *François Mitterrand: The Last French President*. New York: St Martin's Press.

Ungar, Steven (2014) 'Walking with Hegel in Marseilles: Robert Guédiguian and *Les Neiges du Kilimandjaro*', *French Cultural Studies*, 25:3/4, 281–9.

5

Conclusion
Another cinema – a project in time

Throughout this book, I have treated each of Guédiguian's films as a coherent work with its own thematic and narrative specificity. At the same time, it has become clear, and only more so as time progresses, that Guédiguian has been pursuing a continuous project, a conscious collaboration with a group of friends over the past thirty-five years. In conclusion, I would like to step away from individual works and take stock of Guédiguian's career as a holistic practice, as a highly original and remarkably durable project following its own inner logic, one that gives his cinema its particular shape. There are, of course, other cinematic practices that cover long periods of time: Richard Linklater's *Boyhood* (2014), filmed over a twelve-year period of a boy's life, comes to mind, as does Michael Apted's *Up* series. Linklater's 'before/after' trilogy is another interesting experiment in time. There are also many long-term collaborations between directors and actors: François Truffaut and Jean-Pierre Léaud, John Ford and John Wayne and Martin Scorsese and Robert De Niro are good examples, but directors as diverse as the Coen Brothers, Alfred Hitchcock, Ingmar Bergman, John Cassavetes, Akira Kurosawa and many others, have assembled troupes of actors. But Guédiguian's group has far more coherence: his career, like his life, is wholly identified, from the beginning to the present, with this unique group of people; in no other case has the whole been made up so completely by its essential parts.

This project shapes all aspects of Guédiguian's narrative world, starting with the bodies and personalities that appear on screen. First there is Gérard Meylan, Guédiguian's oldest friend. Meylan is an untrained, non-professional actor: a nurse in a pulmonary ward and union representative until his recent retirement, Meylan has acted during vacations and occasional sick leave. In his own film about Guédiguian's work, *Robert sans Robert* (2013), Bernard Sasia, Guédiguian's editor, remembers being struck by Meylan's 'presence' when watching the rushes of *Dernier été*; Guédiguian compares him to John Wayne or Robert Mitchum: untrained actors whose faces 'tell a story' (Danel 2008: 47–8). There is little to distinguish Meylan's personality from his roles: 'Moi, j'ai l'impression qu'il me propose toujours le même rôle, pour lequel il utilise avant tout ma personnalité' (Anon. 2002: 35).[1] Meylan thus points directly towards the world outside of the film images. His pockmarked face, long hair and large frame, slender and smooth in youth but shaped by a lifetime of work, seem a perfect incarnation of an industrial and Mediterranean L'Estaque. His admirable choice of a career helping others, outside the cinema, is representative of a deep moral commitment to his beliefs, a purity that Guédiguian sometimes pushes to intransigence and violence.

Also on screen in Guédiguian's first film is Ariane Ascaride, whose presence virtually guarantees that Guédiguian's fictional world will be centred to some degree on couples and families. Through her, Guédiguian enters into domestic spaces, but he also explores issues concerning gender, especially working women. Her diminutive size, dark hair and Neapolitan origins lend themselves to Madonna-esque characters, saints and whores, but such roles are reconfigured: her mothers are single (*À la vie, à la mort!* for one example), must kill their children (*La Ville est tranquille*) or seize the freedom to pursue their own lives (*Marius et Jeannette*, *Voyage en Arménie*, or *Les Neiges du Kilimandjaro*). Her 'whores' may be pursuing sexual and emotional freedom (*Marie-Jo et ses deux amours*). She is also filmed as a friend among friends, where gender makes no essential difference, as a partner in conversation and action. Ascaride has not only working-class roots but also, perhaps unlike Meylan, a lifelong desire to perform for an audience.[2] As we have seen in *Au fil d'Ariane*, she contributes an acute awareness that the actors are performing for

1 'I feel like he is always offering me the same role, for which he uses my personality.'
2 Her father worked as a hairdresser in Marseilles, but his true calling was as an amateur theatre performer who instilled in his children a love for the stage. (Her brother is a theatre director.)

an audience and that the cinema is a space of encounter above and beyond the particulars of an individual film's narrative.

Jean-Pierre Darroussin, the third easily recognised face in Guédiguian's troupe, appears for the first time in 1985 in *Ki lo sa?* In his early films, he and Pierre Banderet, another classmate of Ascaride from the Conservatory in Paris, take over from older friends and non-professional actors from L'Estaque in earlier work, people such as Hamzaoui, or Jean-Pierre Moreno (Mario) or Djamel Bouanane (Banane) in *Dernier été*.³ But Darroussin can also play a wider range, often in contrast to Meylan: he is soft where Meylan is hard, naïve where Meylan is wary, considerate and compromising where Meylan is authoritarian. They are at times in romantic competition for Ascaride's character. Darroussin also brings a broader palette to Guédiguian's work, shining in comedic roles and able to introduce characters from outside of Marseilles. He often plays contemplative, divided, even fatigued characters, and Sasia notes that he often serves as an alter ego for Guédiguian himself.

Beyond this central core of actors, there are additional recurring faces, often linking the project to broader social contexts. Frédérique Bonnal, Pierre Banderet and Jacques Boudet all make their first appearance in Guédiguian's cinema as early as *Rouge midi*; Alain Lenglet in *Ki lo sa?*; Pascale Roberts in *À la vie, à la mort!* With Bonnal and Banderet, the friendships expand out from the core to a slightly larger community. Bonnal habitually plays a neighbour or the wife of one of the main characters. Banderet (and sometimes Lenglet) also plays representatives of economic power, bankers, CEOs and right-wing villains. Roberts and Boudet are the mouthpieces of a generation older than the core friends, witnesses and connections to a profound history.

The frame is concentrated on these people but also includes objects, spaces and practices that embed them in the social and physical world. In *Robert sans Robert*, Sasia playfully recuts Guédiguian's films to foreground how a number of objects return as repeated motifs. There are important body parts: Ascaride's hairstyles and

---

3 Bouanane has popped up in minor roles in several other films. Hamzaoui has, of course, moved behind the scenes. Guédiguian and Darroussin were friends in Paris, but Guédiguian did not initially want to include Darroussin in films because he did not have a natural accent from L'Estaque.

colours; Meylan's rough face and long hair; Darroussin's receding hairline. There are many objects and actions: clothes, the drinks characters order, recipes, Cézanne's paintings of L'Estaque, the coffee that Meylan or Darroussin will bring to Ascaride in bed, car and truck rides, strike votes with men gathered on the docks, numerous deaths by gunfire. There are recurring spaces: the *bar du centre*, the restaurant of the Perroquet Bleu, particular housing estates, the *crique*, kitchens, even individual alleys and streets that can be recognised from film to film. The music of this particular generation and class provides the soundtrack: a constant flow of kitschy popular hits from past and present; even the classical melodies, often used in poignant or amusing counterpoint (see the fight scene choreographed to Vivaldi in *Marius et Jeannette*), come from popular pieces. Other songs reflect the friends' militant heritage (fight songs from the Spanish revolution or the 'Workers' International') or their theatrical background (Kurt Weil's song, sung by Ascaride in *Au fil d'Ariane*, is also heard in the dump truck in *Dernier été* and in Frisé's shack in *Dieu vomit les tièdes*). On their own, these objects and spaces would have little interest; they become infused with meaning, however, as they play a role in friendships.

In film after film, as the project has unfolded over the years, Guédiguian has necessarily turned to the passing of time as a major theme. Time is inscribed in the changing bodies of the actors as they ineluctably advance in age. As the actors age, new subjects also take priority, spanning their lifetime: love gives way to marriage, then child-rearing, then the desire to continue erotic love and personal renewal. The attempt to find work is replaced by struggles to keep it, unemployment, activism and retirement. Thematic evolution requires newer members in an expanding troupe. Laetitia Pesenti becomes the daughter, to be 'replaced' by Julie-Marie Parmentier, Anaïs Demoustier or Lola Naymark, each with her own personal attributes (sometimes one counterbalancing the other).[4] Younger men usually play boyfriends, co-workers or criminals. Yann Trégouët and Grégoire Leprince-Ringuet exhibit the same anger and intelligence as Guédiguian's male characters in earlier films. At the same time, despite their numerous talents and despite their recurring

4 Pesenti, somewhat like Meylan, has chosen to become a teacher rather than an actress and no longer appears in any films.

appearances, these actresses and actors still, at least for now, play roles that complement the core troupe. It will be a big step if and when an actor accedes into their circle.

The passing of time becomes part of the fabric of Guédiguian's treatment of space and objects as well. Two examples here, both mentioned by Sasia, show Guédiguian's profound archival instincts. The first is well known: the Lafarge cement factory appears first in *Dernier été*, where it is at once the source of work for many of the characters and the imposing, smoking monolith that weighs upon Gilbert when he looks out his bedroom window. In *Rouge midi*, the same factory is again the source of both work and alienation. *Marius et Jeannette* documents its demolition and the characters' regret for the end of a way of life. Later, in *Marie-Jo et ses deux amours*, a sad, post-working-class film, we see the brush reclaiming the site where the factory once stood. The second example is related but demonstrates Guédiguian's eye for details and bodies. In the first shot of his first film, Meylan appears wearing Gilbert's *bleu de travail*, the blue jacket or overalls worn by most French workers. The *bleu de travail* returns in *Rouge midi* where the workers wear them when they strike, when they comfort each other after the death of Salvatore and when they beat up the black-clad fascists hanging posters in the alley. By the time of *Marius et Jeannette*, Dédé, the employed worker, wears just a blue T-shirt; Marius's 'bleu' has turned 'rouge' to reflect his new job as a guard. In *La Ville est tranquille*, Paul wears a light-blue collared shirt when he betrays his striking colleagues and then trades it in for a white shirt to drive the cab. By the time of *Les Neiges du Kilimandjaro*, the bleu de travail is old and wrinkled: Christophe, laid off, wears an aqua-colour running suit. A film like *Le Promeneur du Champ de Mars* contains no blue at all. Neither of these artefacts of long-term loss seems to have been included in a conscious way (though Guédiguian is certainly conscious of them now), but the commitment to this project, this *particular* project, in this place and over time, permits their return, and really their preservation, in film after film.

These effects draw the viewers' attention outwards from the films towards the project and eventually the world itself. Most famously, the tight weave of the films through these actors allows Guédiguian to recycle images from one film to another. We have seen this in *La Ville est tranquille*, when Gérard thinks back to an iconic moment from *Dernier été* before killing himself. It also happens in *À la place du cœur*, when a much younger Darroussin watching the sleeping, nude Ascaride in *Ki lo sa?* There are also still photographs from earlier films included in later ones, such the shots of Darroussin and Ascaride from *Ki lo sa?* found in *Mon père est ingénieur*, one in his wallet and the other framed on her wall. The technique provides continuity through time, but it also gives viewers a glimpse of something beyond the films themselves, a *clin d'œil* towards a relationship that is deeper and larger than the film they are viewing.[5]

When asked if he could not simply form another troupe in the place of these actors, Guédiguian replies, 'Je ne sais pas, mais en tout cas, je n'en constituerai pas d'autre. Et de même que je dis: "les paysages mourront avec moi", cette bande mourra avec moi aussi. Je n'ai pas envie d'en constituer une autre' (Danel 2008: 128).[6] Guédiguian's career is far from over, but it contains within it a logical ending: it will end no earlier and no later than when this friendship does, when they no longer want to continue ('shall we continue?', a question in so many films), or when they die. This unique project, invested in a group of people rather than in an art form or industry, explains why Guédiguian would divide film-makers into those who are 'inside' the cinema (like the Dardenne brothers, whom he admires) and those like him: 'In my relation to the cinema I am inside/outside all of the time' (Danel 2008: 79–80). We enter easily into Guédiguian's narrative world, but we find there an enduring monument to something outside, larger than the cinema, itself just a practice for 'living together as friends'. In this way, Guédiguian's films paradoxically tap into one of the fundamental powers of the cinema itself: its ability to memorialise. 'Le propre du cinéma, c'est le mouvement: puisqu'ils continuent à rire, à pleurer, les acteurs ne meurent pas. Dans les films, Greta Garbo et Marilyn Monroe ne meurent pas' (Danel 2008: 124).[7] Working as he has, Guédiguian has erected a unique and enduring monument to a small number of people and their world.

5 As Guédiguian's career advances, it is remarkable to see how these scenes accomplish the effect of showing characters at various ages that Guédiguian had been grappling with as early as in *Rouge midi*.
6 'I don't know, but in any case, I won't compose another one. And just as I say: "certain landscapes will die with me," this group will die with me too. I have no wish to form another...'
7 'The unique thing about the cinema is movement: since they continue to laugh or cry, actors do not die. In the movies, Greta Garbo and Marilyn Monroe do not die.'

But this monument has a specific if complex quality. Guédiguian's friends are not recorded as passive bodies, in snapshot after snapshot, over the years. They are not preserved simply as personalities either. More precisely, Guédiguian has filmed their active collaboration, the very time that they have shaped by working and thinking together. One can even say that he has filmed their collaborative thinking: in each film, the actors are playing roles, accepting masks and alienation, entering into narratives worlds; in Brechtian fashion, the self-alienation into the role provides a space in which the actors can explore the world, reflect upon it and make creative representations of it. In this way, Guédiguian's films record not only individuals but also the entire set of dynamic practices that have made up their friendships for over thirty-five years.

But why such an immense effort? To 'remain friends for a long time' requires an almost unprecedented commitment, and Guédiguian has had to put up a stubborn resistance to powerful economic forces, to the point of devoting much time to his work as an independent producer in order to fund his film-making. Working so closely, on a daily basis, with one's friends (and one's spouse) is also an extremely fragile endeavour that could come to a sudden and disastrous end with a serious dispute or, heaven forbid, a marital infidelity (making *Marie-Jo et ses deux amours* even more poignant). Moreover, why would viewers, at least 200,000 of them, be so attracted to such a personal project? This is, of course, a fairly small percentage of French film-goers (though the number is much higher for some films), but they are highly loyal to Guédiguian's work, returning to the cinema for every new release. What might be lacking in cultural and political life over the past thirty-five years that would make Guédiguian's sustained exploration of the ins and outs of a friendship a compelling object of contemplation?

The answers to these questions surely involve a desire for something different from how most people live today, at this point in history. If, since the heady days of the 1960s and the militancy of the 1970s, no widespread political action has successfully countered the rise of what is often called neo-liberalism, with its cultural figures of the entrepreneur and the consumer, Guédiguian's films offers a different choice, an anchor of resistance. They offer figures of the complex and profound friendships that we have been calling *philia*: models of human interaction that instead value conversation, difference, equality and commitment; that weave our lives into a temporal fabric combining past, present and future; that intertwine them with the lives of others; that help us determine what we think of as virtuous and worthwhile; that acknowledge our vulnerability; that give meaning to the seemingly banal spaces and everyday objects that surround us; that encourage us to be invested in our city and the broader world in which we live; and that open us up to difference and dynamic change. In a time shaped by cultural figures that breed solitude, displacement, immediate gratification and future investment, Guédiguian's cinema memorialises, for now and for the future, examples of how we might live different and, perhaps, more flourishing lives.

References

Anonymous (2002) '*À la vie, à l'amour:* interview avec Jean-Pierre Darroussin, Gérard Meylan, et Ariane Ascaride', *Télérama*, 26 June, pp. 32–6.

Danel, Isabelle (2008) *Conversation avec Robert Guédiguian*, Paris: Les Carnets de l'Info.

Kantcheff, Christophe (2013) *Robert Guédiguian, cinéaste*, Paris: Éditions du Chêne.

Filmography

Dernier été *(1981)*

80 minutes
Production: René Féret, Les Films Arquebuse
Screenplay: Robert Guédiguian and Frank Le Wita
Photography: Gilberto Azevedo
Editing: Vincent Pinel
Assistant directors: Bruno Domercq and Bernard Sasia
Sound: Luc Perini
Production Manager: Michelle Plaa
Principal actors: Gérard Meylan (Gilbert), Ariane Ascaride (Josiane), Jean-Pierre Moreno (Mario), Djamal Bouanane (Banane), Malek Hamzaoui (Le Muet), Joëlle Modola (Martine), Jim Sortino (Boule)

Rouge midi *(completed in 1983, presented at Cannes 1984, released 1985)*

110 minutes
Production: Patricia Moraz, Alain Dahan, Robert Guédiguian, Abilène Productions, Col.Ima.Son
Screenplay: Robert Guédiguian and Frank Le Wita
Photography: Gilberto Azevedo
Editing: Catherine Poitevin
Assistant director: Bernard Sasia
Sound: Antoine Ouvrier
Production Manager: Alain Dahan

Principal actors: Gérard Meylan (Jérôme, Sauveur), Ariane Ascaride (Maggiorina), Raoul Gimenez (Mindou), Martine Drai (Ginette), Pierre Pradinas (Pierre), Frédérique Bonnal (Céline), Abdel Ali Sid (young Sauveur), Djamal Bouanane (Salvatore), Salvatore Condro (Guido), Jacques Boudet (Fredou), Pierre Banderet (factory owner)

Ki lo sa? *(1985, undistributed)*

86 minutes
Production: Édouard Bobrowski, Robert Guédiguian, Col.Ima.Son
Screenplay: Robert Guédiguian
Photography: Gilberto Azevedo
Editing: Bernard Sasia
Assistant director: Bernard Sasia
Sound: Henri-Claude Mariani
Principal actors: Jean-Pierre Darroussin (Dada), Ariane Ascaride (Marie/Charlot), Gérard Meylan (Gitan), Pierre Banderet (Pierrot), Alain Lenglet (Marie's client)

Dieu vomit les tièdes *(completed in 1989, released 1991)*

100 minutes
Production: Alain Guesnier, Yvon Davis, Gilles Sandoz, Robert Guédiguian – CDN Production and Agat Films & Cie
Screenplay: Robert Guédiguian and Sophie Képès
Photography: Bernard Cavalié
Editing: Bernard Sasia
Sound: Philippe Combes and Laurent Lafran
Production Manager: Malek Hamzaoui
Principal actors: Jean-Pierre Darroussin (Cochise), Gérard Meylan (Frisé), Ariane Ascaride (Tirelire), Pierre Banderet (Quatre-Œil), Hélène Surgère (Cochise's mother), Jacques Boudet (Fernand), Farouk Bermouga (Karim); David Minassian, David Savelli, Magali Meylan, and Stéphane Harrouche (the characters as children)

L'Argent fait le bonheur *(broadcast on France 2, 1993)*

85 minutes
Production: Caméras Continentals, France 2, Centre National du Cinéma de l'Image Animée

Screenplay: Robert Guédiguian and Jean-Louis Milesi
Photography: Bernard Cavalié
Editing: Bernard Sasia
Sound: Laurent Laffran
Production Managers: Malek Hamzaoui and Victor Beniard
Principal actors: Jean-Pierre Darroussin (the priest), Ariane Ascaride (Simona Viali), Jean-Jérôme Esposito (Pierre Viali), Pierre Banderet (Degros), Fédérique Bonnal (Madame Degros), Marilyn Nobili-Grégorio (Isabelle Degros), Gérard Meylan (Muñoz), Lorella Cravotta (Madame Muñoz), Jacques Boutet (Godre), Malek Hamzaoui (Amzoula), Michèle Addala (Madame Amzoula), Abdel Ali Sid (Mourad), Marcel Bluwal (Viali)

À la vie, à la mort! *(1995)*

100 minutes
Production: Agat Films & Cie
Screenplay: Robert Guédiguian and Jean-Louis Milesi
Photography: Bernard Cavalié
Editing: Bernard Sasia
Sound: Laurent Lafran
Production Manager: Malek Hamzaoui
Principal actors: Ariane Ascaride (Marie-Sol), Gérard Meylan (José), Jean-Pierre Darroussin (Jaco), Jacques Gamblin (Patrick), Pascale Roberts (Josépha), Jacques Boudet (Papa Carlosa), Jacques Pieiller (Otto), Farid Ziane (Farid), Laetitia Pesenti (Vénus), Frédérique Bonnal (Jaco's wife), Alain Lenglet (Marie-Sol's boss), Pierre Banderet (the television talking head)

Marius et Jeannette (1997)

102 minutes
Production: Agat Films & Cie, La Sept Cinéma, Canal+
Screenplay: Robert Guédiguian and Jean-Louis Milesi
Photography: Bernard Cavalié
Editing: Berard Sasia
Sound: Laurent Lafran
Production Manager: Malek Hamaoui
Principal actors: Ariane Ascaride (Jeannette), Gérard Meylan (Marius), Pascale Roberts (Caroline), Jacques Boudet (Justin), Frédérique

Bonnal (Monique), Jean-Pierre Darroussin (Dédé), Laetitia Pesenti (Magali), Miloud Nacer (Malek), Pierre Banderet (Ebrard)

À la place du cœur *(1998)*

113 minutes
Production: Agat Films & Cie, La Sept Cinéma, France 2 Cinéma, Canal+
Screenplay: Robert Guédiguian and Jean-Louis Milesi, adapted from James Baldwin's *If Beale Street Could Talk*
Photography: Bernard Cavalié
Editing: Bernard Sasia
Sound: Lauran Lafran
Production Manager: Malek Hamzaoui
Principal actors: Ariane Ascaride (Mariane), Jean-Pierre Darroussin (Joël), Gérard Meylan (Frank), Laure Raoust (Clim), Alexandre Ogou (Bébé), Christine Brücher (Francine), Pierre Banderet (the lawyer), Jacques Boudet (Mr Levy), Jacques Pieiller (the cop), Beata Nilska (Madame Radic), Marius Grygielewicz (Piet Radic)

À l'attaque! *(2000)*

90 minutes
Production: Agat Films & Cie, Diaphana, TF1 Films Productions, Canal+
Screenplay: Robert Guédiguian and Jean-Louis Milesi
Photography: Bernard Cavalié
Editing: Bernard Sasia
Sound: Laurent Lafran
Production Manager: Malek Hamzaoui
Principal actors: Ariane Ascaride (Lola), Jacques Boudet (Pépé Moliterno), Jean-Pierre Darroussin (Jean-Do), Gérard Meylan (Gigi), Frédérique Bonnal (Marthe), Denis Podalydès (Yvan), Jacques Pieiller (Xavier), Patrick Bonnel (Henri, the lazy guy), Pierre Banderet (Moreau), Christine Brücher (Madame Moreau), Pascale Roberts (Henri's mother), Laetitia Pesenti (Vanessa)

La Ville est tranquille *(2001)*

143 minutes
Production: Agat Films & Cie, Diaphan, Canal+

Screenplay: Robert Guédiguian and Jean-Louis Milesi
Photography: Bernard Cavalié
Editing: Bernard Sasia
Sound: Laurent Lafran
Production Manager: Malek Hamazoui
Principal actors: Ariane Ascaride (Michèle), Jean-Pierre Darroussin (Paul), Pierre Banderet (Claude), Gérard Meylan (Gérard), Julie-Marie Parmentier (Fiona), Véronique Balme (Ameline), Christine Brücher (Viviane Froment), Jacques Pieiller (Yves Froment), Jacques Boudet (Paul's father), Pascale Roberts (Paul's mother), Julien Sevan Papazian (the piano player)

Marie-Jo et ses deux amours *(2002)*

124 minutes
Production: Agat Films & Cie, France 3 Cinéma, Canal+
Screenplay: Robert Guédiguian and Jean-Louis Milesi
Photography: Renato Berta
Editing: Bernard Sasia
Sound: Laurent Lafran
Production Manager: Malek Hamzaoui
Principal actors: Ariane Ascaride (Marie-Jo), Jean-Pierre Darroussin (Daniel), Gérard Meylan (Marco), Julie-Marie Parmentier (Julie), Yann Trégouët (Sylvain)

Mon père est ingénieur *(2004)*

108 minutes
Production: Agat Films & Cie, France 3 Cinéma, Mikros Image, Grimages Films
Screenplay: Robert Guédiguian and Jean-Louis Milesi
Photography: Renato Berta
Editing: Bernard Sasia
Sound: Laurent Lafran
Production Manager: Malek Hamzaoui
Principal actors: Ariane Ascaride (Natacha/Marie), Jean-Pierre Darroussin (Jérémie/Joseph), Gérard Meylan (Vadino/Roustido), Pascale Roberts (Natacha's mother), Jacques Boudet (Natacha's father), Mathilda Duthu (Mylène/Mireille), Youssef Sahbeddine (Rachid/Vincent), Frédérique Bonnal (Natacha's neighbour)

Le Promeneur du Champ de Mars *(2005)*

117 minutes
Production: Film Oblige, Agat Films & Cie, Arte France Cinéma
Screenplay: Gilles Taurand and Georges-Marc Benamou, adapted from Benamou's *Le Dernier Mitterrand*
Photography: Renato Berta
Editing: Bernard Sasia
Sound: Laurent Lafran
Principal actors: Michel Bouquet (François Mitterrand), Jalil Lespert (Antoine Moreau), Anne Canineau (Jeanne), Sarah Grappin (Judith)

Le Voyage en Arménie *(2006)*

125 minutes
Principal Production: Agat Films & Cie, France 3 Cinéma, Canal+
Screenplay: Ariane Ascaride, Marie Desplechin and Robert Guédiguian
Photography: Pierre Milon
Editing: Bernard Sasia
Sound: Laurent Lafran
Production Manager: Malek Hamzaoui
Principal actors: Ariane Ascaride (Anna), Gérard Meylan (Yervanth), Chorik Grigorian (Schaké), Roman Avinian (Manouk), Simon Abkarian (Sarkis Arabian), Jean-Pierre Darroussin (Pierre), Madeleine Guédiguian (Jeannette), Jalil Lespert (Simon), Marcel Bluwal (Barsam)

Lady Jane *(2008)*

102 minutes
Production: Agat Films & Cie
Screenplay: Robert Guédiguian and Jean-Louis Milesi
Photography: Pierre Milon
Editing: Bernard Sasia
Sound: Laurent Lafran
Production Manager: Malek Hamzaoui
Principal actors: Ariane Ascaride (Muriel), Gérard Meylan (René), Jean-Pierre Darroussin (François), Jacques Boudet (Henri), Pascale Roberts (Solange), Yann Trégouët (Agostini's son)

L'Armée du crime *(2009)*

139 minutes
Production: Agat Films & Cie, StudioCanal, France 3 Cinéma
Screenplay: Robert Guédiguian, Serge Le Perón, Gilles Taurand
Photography: Pierre Milon
Editing: Bernard Sasia
Sound: Laurent Lafran
Production Manager: Malek Hamzaoui
Principal actors: Simon Abkarian (Missak Manouchian), Virginie Ledoyen (Mélinée Manouchian), Robinson Stévenin (Marcel Rayman), Lola Naymark (Monique Stern), Grégoire Leprince-Ringuet (Thomas Elek), Adrien Jolivet (Henri Krasucki), Olga Legrand (Olga Bancic), Jean-Pierre Darroussin (Inspector Pujol), Yann Trégouët (Commissioner David), Ariane Ascaride (Madame Elek), Gérard Meylan (a cop in the Resistance)

Les Neiges du Kilimandjaro *(2011)*

90 minutes
Production: Agat Films & Cie, France 3 Cinéma, Canal+
Screenplay: Robert Guédiguian and Jean-Louis Milesi, inspired by Victor Hugo's poem, 'Les Pauvres Gens'
Photography: Pierre Milon
Editing: Bernard Sasia
Sound: Laurent Lafran
Production Manager: Malek Hamzaoui
Principal actors: Ariane Ascaride (Marie-Claire), Jean-Pierre Darroussin (Michel), Gérard Meylan (Raoul), Marilyne Canto (Denise), Grégoire Leprince-Ringuet (Christophe), Anaïs Demoustier (Flo), Julie-Marie Parmentier (Agnès)

Au fil d'Ariane *(2014)*

Production: Agat Films & Cie, Canal+, Centre National du Cinéma de l'Image Animée, Chaocorp
Screenplay: Robert Guédiguian and Serge Valleti
Photography: Pierre Milon
Editing: Bernard Sasia and Armelle Mahé
Production Manager: Malek Hamzaoui

Principal actors: Ariane Ascaride (Ariane), Gérard Meylan (Denis), Jean-Pierre Darroussin (taxi driver and theatre director), Jacques Boudet (Jacques the poet), Anaïs Demoustier (Martine and the actress), Youssouf Djaoro (Martial), Adrien Jolivet (Raphaël), Lola Naymark (Lola)

Une histoire de fou *(2015)*

Production: Agat Films & Cie, France 3 Cinéma, Alvy Productions, Canal+
Screenplay: Robert Guédiguian and Gilles Taurand, based on the autobiography of José Antonio Gurriarán
Photography: Pierre Milon
Editing: Bernard Sasia
Sound: Laurent Lafran
Production Manager: Jinane Dagher (Lebanon)
Principal actors: Simon Abkarian (Hovannès Alexandrian), Ariane Ascaride (Anouch Alexandrian), Grégoire Leprince-Ringuet (Gilles Teissier)

Select bibliography

For interviews and critical works on Guédiguian's films, see the References sections for each chapter.

Books on Robert Guédiguian

The present volume is the first scholarly monograph on Guédiguian's work. The three books that have previously appeared, all in French, were written by professional journalists. Two of them are made up of extensive interviews with the film-maker.

Danel, Isabelle (2008) *Conversation avec Robert Guédiguian*, Paris: Les Carnets de l'Info.

Written by a film journalist and friend of Guédiguian, and so without pretentions to objectivity. Valuable information throughout, especially on Guédiguian's youth, years in the political party and reactions to criticisms of his films. Also contains perceptive commentary on each film made before 2008.

Kantcheff, Christophe (2013) *Robert Guédiguian, cinéaste*, Paris: Editions du Chêne.

A large, beautifully presented volume, written with access to extensive documentation from Guédiguian himself. Copiously illustrated with stills from Guédiguian's films, set photos, family albums and current photographs of areas where Guédiguian's films are set. Also includes in-depth interviews with Meylan, Ascaride and Darroussin. A well-written, thematic, critical approach.

Sahuc, Stéphane (2011) *Parlons politique: Maryse Dumas-Robert Guédiguian*, Paris: Les Éditions Arcane-17.

A three-way interview book between the author, Guédiguian and Maryse Dumas, former postal worker and highly placed trade-union leader in the Confédération Générale du Travail, having appeared in a series devoted to 'reconstructing the left'. Provides valuable insight into Guédiguian's attitude towards political shifts since the 1970s.

Book chapters and journal articles

Readers seeking more analytic and scholarly approaches will find several helpful articles and book chapters, mostly on individual films.

Anderson, Philip (2008) 'Stories of Violence, Violence of History: The Political Logic of Guédiguian's Cinema from *Dernier été* (1980) to *La Ville est tranquille* (2001)', *The Australian Journal of French Studies*, 45:3, 238–49.

Cortade, Ludovic (2009) 'The Spatial Evacuation of Politics: Landscape, Power and the "Monarch" in Robert Guédiguian's *The Last Mitterrand*', *Yale French Studies*, 115: 67–79.

Mariette, Audrey (2006), 'Ressources et contraintes d'un passé militant: le cas d'un cinéaste "engagé", Robert Guédiguian', in Sylvie Tissot, Christophe Gaubert and Marie-Hélène Lechien (eds.), *Reconversions militantes*, Limoges: Pulim, pp. 201–29.

McGonagle, Joseph (2007) 'The End of an Era: Marseilles at the Millennium in Robert Guédiguian's *La Ville est tranquille* (2001)', *Studies in French Cinema*, 7:3, 231–41.

O'Shaughnessy, Martin (2008) *The New Face of Political Cinema*, New York: Berghahn Books.

Ouesselin, Edward (2007) 'Un Conte politisé: *À l'attaque!* de Robert Guédiguian', *The French Review*, 81:1, 124–34.

Powrie, Phil (2001) '*Marius et Jeannette*: Nostalgia and Utopia', in Lucy Mazdon (ed.), *France on Film: Reflections on Popular French Cinema*, London: Wallflower, pp. 133–44.

Rascaroli, Laura (2006) 'The Place of the Heart: Scaling Spaces in Robert Guédiguian's Cinema', *Studies in French Cinema*, 6:2, 95–105.

Ungar, Steven (2000), '*Marius et Jeannette*: A Political Tale', *IRIS*, 29:spring, 39–52.

—— (2014) 'Walking with Hegel in Marseilles: Robert Guédiguian and *Les Neiges du Kilimandjaro*', *French Cultural Studies*, 25:3/4, 281–9.

Index

Abkarian, Simon 110, 114–15
Agat Films & Cie 1, 45, 54, 60
A la place du cœur 71–6, 77–8, 86–8, 91, 95, 101, 140
A la vie, à la mort! 53–9, 61, 76–7, 82, 91, 94, 99, 129, 136–7
alienation effect 33–4, 130
    see also Brecht, Bertolt
Anderson, Philip 9, 24–5, 86–7, 92
apocalyptic view of history 9, 44, 87, 92
Apted, Michael 135
L' Argent fait le bonheur, 49–53
Aristotle 10–15, 22, 45
    Nicomachean Ethics 10–15
Armée du crime, L' 43, 114–18
Armstrong, Louis 73
Ascaride, Ariane 5, 10, 22, 25, 34, 40, 45, 50, 52, 54, 59, 61, 72, 74–6, 80–3, 87, 92, 96, 100–2, 110, 114, 118, 120, 128–32, 134, 136–40
Atalante, L' (1934) 99

Aubrac, Raymond 116n.17
Au fil d'Ariane 128–32, 138
Aurelius, Marcus 31

Badiou, Alain 9, 109–14
Baldwin, James 71–2
    If Beale Street Could Talk 71–8
Banderet, Pierre 10, 34, 40, 45, 54, 76, 82, 87, 101, 137
Bazin, André 64n.15
Bégaudeau, François 104–8
Belmondo, Jean-Paul 30
Benamou, Georges-Marc 103–6
Benjamin, Walter 33
Bergman, Ingmar 135
Berta, Renato 97n.4, 101, 106
Besson, Luc 20
Bloch, Ernst 35, 45, 51–3, 100–2
Bonnal, Frédérique 33, 45, 51, 65, 83, 137
Bonnel, Patrick 101
Borsalino (1970) 30
Borsalino & Cie (1974) 30
Bouanane, Djamel 21, 137

Boudet, Jacques 10, 43, 45, 55, 64, 76, 89, 91, 122, 129, 147
Bouloque, Sylvain 116–17
Bouquet, Michel 104–7
Boyhood (2014) 135
Braque, Georges 26
Brecht, Bertolt 33, 38, 49, 50, 75, 130–1, 141
  A Short Organum for the Theatre 33
Breton, André 36–7
Brücher, Christine 72

Cahiers du cinéma 71, 105
Cannes film festival 33, 59–60, 71, 75, 118
Capra, Frank 52
Carné, Marcel 58
Cassavetes, John 135
Cavalié, Bernard 42, 45
Cézanne, Paul 26–7, 70, 138
Char, René 36–8
Chaunu, Pierre 41
Chirac, Jacques 59–60
Cocker, Joe 125
Coen Brothers 135
colour, use of 16, 66, 68, 70, 88, 95, 97, 101, 106, 118, 129, 130–1, 138–9
Common Programme of Government 2, 7, 123
communism 4–9, 9, 16, 20, 31, 39–44, 48–9, 52, 64–6, 70, 95, 100–3, 109–17, 123, 126, 128n.29
  anti-communism 6–7, 39–41

community politics 17, 48, 60, 62, 100–2, 108–9
Confédération Générale de Travail (CGT) 5
consumer (cultural figure) 14–16, 54, 110, 141
conte de l'Estaque 17, 43, 47, 57, 73, 76, 78, 85
conversation 12–13, 19, 21–5, 48, 65, 69, 117, 124, 136, 141
Cooper, John M. 111n.9, 12
Cortade, Ludovic 105–8
Courtois, Stéphane 116–17
Crime de Monsieur Lange, Le (1936) 64
Curtius, Ernst Robert 35

Danel, Pascal 124n.24
Dante 98
Dardenne brothers 140
Darroussin, Jean-Pierre 10, 34, 38, 45, 49, 55, 65, 72, 74–6, 81–2, 89, 94, 96, 100–2, 114, 118, 120, 123, 130, 132, 137, 138, 140
Davis, Yvon 45
Delon, Alain 30
Demoustier, Anaïs 130, 138
Demy, Jacques 77
De Niro, Robert 135
Dernier été 20–8, 32, 34, 36, 48, 64, 69, 70, 73, 80–1, 92, 94–5, 136–9
Derobert, Eric 38, 70n.24
Desplat, Alexandre 37–8
Desplechin, Arnaud 60

Dieu vomit les tièdes 38–45, 48–9, 83, 91–2, 138
Diva (1981) 20
Duvivier, Julien 76
Dylan, Bob 38

eating *see* meal scenes
editing, use of 16, 63, 67, 87, 97, 105
Ekberg, Anita 131n.31
Engels, Friedrich 5, 95
Enrico, Robert 40
entrepreneur (cultural figure) 14–16, 54, 141
L'Estaque 2–6, 16–20, 23–33, 40, 47, 53–7, 61–2, 70–9, 85, 89, 93, 103, 119, 123, 129, 136–7, 138
eudaimonia see flourishing

Fassbinder, Rainer Werner 75n.27
Fellini, Frederico 131n.31
Ferran, Pascale 60
Ferré, Léo 115
fiction de gauche 2
figures (cultural figuration) 14–17, 74, 85, 94, 109, 114, 141–2
film bilan 36–7, 123
flourishing 10–11, 51, 53, 142
Ford, John 135
French Revolution 38–48
Fresnay, Pierre 62
Friedman, Milton 15
friendship 2–3, 9–24, 25–30, 35–8, 44, 48, 50, 55–6, 59, 69, 71, 85–6, 93, 102–3, 110–14, 127, 130, 137–41
character friendship 11, 13
and cinematic representation 12
and meaning in life 11–12, 19, 23, 37, 64, 66, 138, 142
of pleasure 12–13, 16, 21
and time 15–17, 21
of utility 10–11, 16
Frodon, Jean-Michel 75n.27
Front National 41, 48, 61, 65, 67, 71, 126
Fukuyama, Francis 8
Furet, François 6–9, 39–41

Gamblin, Jacques 54
Garbo, Greta 140
Gaudí, Antoni 69
Girard, René 119–21
globalisation 4, 62–5, 70, 104, 109–10
Gospel According to Saint Matthew, The (1964) 130
Goudet, Stéphane 70n.24
Goya, Francisco 56
Guesnier, Alain 45

Hamzaoui, Malek 10, 21, 32, 45, 50, 61, 69, 100, 137
Haupt, Georges 5–7
Heffron, Richard 40
Histoire de fou, Une 118n.20
history 2–9, 14, 16, 19, 25–6, 32–5, 40, 47–8, 70, 75, 85, 87–9, 92–5, 125–6
Hitchcock, Alfred 135

Hugo, Victor 108, 127
  Les Misérables 31
  'Les pauvres gens' 127

Jameson, Fredric 100, 102
Jaurès, Jean 123, 126
Jolivet, Adrien 129
Jospin, Lionel 60

Kaganski, Serge 88–9, 92
Kantcheff, Christophe 5n.6, 96, 101
Kaplan, Steven L. 41
Ki lo sa? 34–8, 45, 48, 64, 74, 75, 102, 137
Kurosawa, Akira 135

Lady Jane 10, 85, 118–22, 123
Léaud, Jean-Pierre 135
Lefebvre, Georges 39
Légitime défense (1982) 28n.7
Lenglet, Alain 34, 45, 88, 137
Le Péron, Serge 114
Leprince-Ringuet, Grégoire 138
Lespert, Jalil 104
Le Wita, Frank 103
Linklater, Richard 135
local politics *see* community politics

Manichean tendencies in Guédiguian's films 2, 75
Manouchian, Missak 114–18
Marie-Jo et ses deux amours 94–9, 139, 141
Marius (1931) 21n.2, 62, 124
Marius et Jeannette 2, 4, 21, 58, 59–71, 75–7, 83, 87, 95, 123, 136, 138, 139

Marseilles 2–5, 10, 26, 30–2, 41, 54, 62, 65, 72–3, 86–8, 100, 106, 108, 118–22, 129–31, 136, 137
Marx, Karl and Marxism 2–3, 5, 7, 9, 10, 24, 39, 48, 100, 109, 131
  The German Ideology 2–3
mask (as theme) 20, 64, 85, 118–22, 124, 126, 132, 141
Mastroianni, Marcello 131n.31
Mathiez, Albert 39
May, Todd 14–16
meal scenes 58, 67–9, 104
Meylan, Gérard 5, 8–10, 20–1, 26–8, 33–4, 40–1, 45, 50, 54, 61, 72, 76, 77, 90, 92, 94, 96, 100–1, 114, 118, 120, 123, 129, 135–9
Milesi, Jean-Louis 49, 61–2
Militantisme de proximité *see* community politics
Mitchum, Robert 136
Mitterrand, François 7–9, 19, 103–14
Monroe, Marilyn 140
Montaigne, Michel de 12, 13, 17, 21
monument making, cinema as 14, 70, 87, 140–1
Moreau, Jeanne 64
Moreno, Jean-Pierre 21, 137
Morris, William 31, 95–6
Murat, Joachim 56
music, use of 22, 37–8, 44, 49, 54, 77, 86, 110, 113, 115, 120, 122, 138

Napoléon, Joseph 56
Naymark, Lola 129, 138

Nehamas, Alexander 12–13
Neiges du Kilimandjaro, Les 2n.1, 7, 123–8, 136

Ogou, Alexandre 71, 74, 88
O'Shaughnessy, Martin 8–9, 47, 78
Ozouf, Monique 39–40

Pagnol, Marcel 12, 21, 57, 62, 124
Panossian, Razmik 108, 112
Parmentier, Julie-Marie 87, 90, 138
Pasolini, Pier Paolo 20, 21, 24, 25, 130
  Scritti Corsari 24
  Una vita violenta 20
Pasqua and Debré laws 60
Péguy, Charles 105
Péron, Didier 75
Pesenti, Laetitia 55, 76, 138
philia see friendship
Pieiller, Jacques 45, 55, 72, 77
Podalydès, Denis 77
Powrie, Phil 60, 62, 69, 75
project over time, Guédiguian's cinema as 2, 16, 17, 19, 75, 85, 102, 123, 135–42
Promeneur du Champs de Mars, Le 103–8, 114, 118, 139

Quai des brumes, Le (1938) 58

Raoust, Laure 71, 74
Rascaroli, Laura 54, 64, 73, 88
religion 40, 44, 59, 65n.17, 70n.23, 101–2
Renoir, Jean 29, 40n.13, 42, 64

resistance (theme) 9, 48, 51, 53, 55, 58–9, 65, 67, 91, 100, 102, 117–18
re-use of scenes from previous films 75, 102, 140
Révolution française, La (1989) 40
Roberts, Pascale 54, 60, 65, 77, 83, 101, 122, 137
Robespierre 39, 41, 43
Rorty, Amélia 13
Rossini, Gioachino 50
Rouge midi 4, 28–34, 45, 48, 89, 94–5, 131, 137, 139, 140

Sahuc, Stéphane 8, 14, 47–8, 60
Sandoz, Gilles 45
sans-papiers see undocumented workers
Sarkozy, Nicolas 104n.11, 109–10
Sasia, Bernard 45, 136–9
Satie, Erik 86, 93
Schapiro, Meyer 26
Scorsese, Martin 135
Sirk, Douglas 75n.27
Skorecki, Louis 75n.27
songs, use of popular or political 38, 43, 55, 58, 62, 68, 124, 131, 138
Sotinel, Thomas 86
Standing, Guy 55n.5, 125–6
stocktaking film *see film bilan*

Taurand, Gilles 103
Telfer, Elizabeth 11, 13
Tiersky, Ronald 7, 103
Tissot, Sylvie 10
Toni (1935) 29, 40n.13, 42

Trégouët, Yann 91, 138
Truffaut, François 64, 135
Tulard, Jean 40

undocumented workers 59–61
unemployment and underemployment 4, 8, 26, 41, 55–6, 62, 65, 70, 88, 100, 123–7
Ungar, Steven 61–2, 125
Utopianism 1, 17, 31, 35–8, 48, 51–3, 57, 62, 64, 70, 74, 78, 85–6, 94–9 *passim*, 101–2

vengeance (theme)
Vigo, Jean 99
Ville est tranquille, La 27, 86–94, 136, 139
Vivaldi, Antonio 20, 28, 57, 138
Voyage en Arménie 108–14, 118, 136

Wayne, John 135–6
Weill, Kurt 130–1, 138

Ziane, Farid 55
Zola, Émile 3–4, 26, 106
 Germinal 106
 Naïs Micoulin 3–4

EU authorised representative for GPSR:
Easy Access System Europe, Mustamäe tee 50,
10621 Tallinn, Estonia
gpsr.requests@easproject.com

www.ingramcontent.com/pod-product-compliance
Lightning Source LLC
Chambersburg PA
CBHW070359240426
43671CB00013BA/2563